"*Unwrapping the Gift of Communication* is a gift to its readers. A gift to unwrap and to use. A gift, offering biblically informed, research-based strategies for communicating in ways that truly serve others and honor our Lord Jesus Christ. I can't wait to use this gift in my courses! And I can't wait to hear how others—whether students, church study groups, or individual Christians—benefit from the wisdom in this book."

—**Diane M. Badzinski**, Chair, Professor of Communication, Colorado Christian University

"As a longtime communication professor and practitioner, and now as a pastor in a large, nondenominational church, I find Dr. Jones's work here to be extremely valuable, relevant, and practical. Many of the real-life stories and illustrations noted in this book seem to be replicated in my world on a regular basis in modern ministry life. More than ever, it seems that communication misunderstandings abound, but this text not only addresses many of those challenges, but also provides practical, time-tested wisdom from God's word."

—**John Buckles**, Group Life and Connection Pastor, Heritage Christian Church Columbus, Ohio

"As one who has taught communication in Christian institutions of higher education for close to 40 years, this book is an amazing blessing. It tells the story of the beautiful relationship between scriptural principles and the academic study of communication. Jones provides insightful observations and practical applications of the communication principles that all followers of Christ should seek to emulate so that we can better reflex the love of our Savior to a world that so desperately needs it."

—**Tom Carmody**, Vanguard University

"*Unwrapping the Gift of Communication* provides readers with a biblical perspective on relationships and untangles some of the intricacies of human interaction. Using sound theory, personal anecdotes, and discussion-based questions, Dr. Jones carefully considers the function and impact of messages and describes a Christ-centered approach to communication. An inspiring text with many great lessons!

—**Charles Choi**, Pepperdine University

"Kevin does a nice job of taking some fairly intricate communication theories and making them relatable and understandable to non-academics. The personal examples are poignant and very nice ways of illustrating the theories. Kevin has also done a nice job of finding scriptural passages that make a connection between the theory and our faith walk."

—**Konrad Hack**, Concordia University

"A gift to Christian college students and other Christ-followers, Jones's book stands out for its pairing of ancient biblical wisdom with contemporary communication theories, its blend of academic and pastoral voices, and the author's personable/vulnerable voice. Prioritizing personal application, each chapter carefully unpacks one key concept from communication theory and one key Bible passage (or section of Scripture), followed by suggested ways to put these insights into practice and questions for self-reflection. The book's approachability is a natural outflow of the author's transparency, his heart for fellow learners, and his passion for communication practices that reflect the Creator's design."

—**John B. Hatch**, Retired Professor, Eastern University; CCSN Senior Fellow

"Dr. Jones has written a practical and insightful book for understanding God's unique gift of communication. He provides wise relational principles and helpful examples from Scripture and life experiences. This book could be a great tool as a small group study, with married or premarital couples, or for anyone wanting to build better communication skills!"

—**Mike Parks**, Senior Pastor, Independence First Baptist Church, Independence, Oregon

Unwrapping the Gift of Communication

Unwrapping the Gift of Communication

Theoretical Applications and Biblical Wisdom for
Relationships that Thrive

int

KEVIN T. JONES

FOREWORD BY Diane M. Badzinski

Integratio Press
Pasco, Washington

Dedications

First, and foremost, to Yahweh, for giving us the gift of communication. Your gift allows us to be made in your likeness and navigate our journeys, and for that I am thankful.

For Jack Hibbs, Senior Pastor, Calvary Chapel Chino Hills, California. You believed in me when no one else did and you started me on this journey. (Even though you had no idea that God used you to do so.)

For the hundreds of students over the years who have helped me explore and develop the content in this book. Reading your papers inspired many of the ideas in this book. Thank you for contributing to this journey.

Most importantly, for Michelle, my bride, and my partner. Without you, this journey would have no meaning or purpose. I do not know who I would be without you.

Table of Contents

Acknowledgments

First, i must acknowledge and thank my COMM 480 Senior Capstone Class from the fall semester 2017. This book was born from many of our class discussions and conversations. Many of your ideas have made their way onto these pages. Thank you, Brittany, Libby, Haley, Ashlie, Maddie, Samantha, Dalis, Alex, and Rachel. I loved sitting with all of you upstairs in Minthorn Hall, drinking coffee, and sharing our journey together. I miss you all.

Second, thank you to my prayer team, Mike Crosby, Charles Choi, Gregg Lamm, and Jonathan Anderegg. You have shown me what a true friend is, and I could not have survived this project without your prayers and support. Thank you for letting me send you regular prayer request updates and for letting me share my journey with you. Thank you for being honest, even when it was not easy for me to hear what you had to say. You have all made this a better book. Thank you for your lives that have role modeled for me what healthy, Godly communication looks like. Each one of you is present in this book in many ways.

Thank you to the administration of George Fox University for giving me the sabbatical I needed to focus on finishing this book. Thank you, Steve Classen, for holding down the fort in my absence so I could take my sabbatical and not worry too much about the department falling apart.

Thank you to Robert Woods for believing in this book and supporting this project every step of the way. Thank you for publishing this book and for your editorial oversight throughout the process. Thank you for your commitment to develop a press that supports quality scholarly materials from a Christian faith-integration perspective. May this book, and many others in your press, serve the next generation of Christian educators. May the Lord bless you and keep you.

A special thank you to John Hatch for speaking your wisdom, insight, suggestions, and thoughts, and for all your contributions that made this book much, much better. If this book is successful in any way, it will be because of your contributions. Thank you also to Tom Carmody for your help. Much of what is in this book about Christ-like communication you have role modeled to me over the years with your life.

Thank you to Bethany Widdecomb for your editorial help on earlier drafts of this book. Thank you to Sally Hopkins, for guiding me through this journey we call life. Thank you, Arielle Leonard-Hodges, for your kind insights and thoughts that helped make the book stronger. Crystal Head-rick, I could not have done this without your grammar skills. And thank you to Evan Eisenbeis for your help with researching some challenging topics. And thank you to the many people who have reviewed chapters or portions of these essays over the years: Robin Jones Gunn, Steve Classen, Charles Choi, Konrad Hack, Mike Parks, John Buckles, and other reviewers. And thank you to my family (Michelle, Susi, Gabi, Sami, and Kaleb) for letting me use so many of your stories in this book to illustrate our journey with communication (for better or worse).

Foreword

I RECEIVED A GIFT FROM MY DAUGHTER. It came in a small crème-colored box with an elegant black bow. Inside was a lovely candle. "It's a Jo Malone London candle," my daughter exclaimed. I didn't want to burn such an expensive candle, so I put the gift back in its box. Unless I change my mind, the candle will never serve its intended purpose.

Communication is a gift. Yet, I wonder how often we fail to use the gift as God intended. We keep quiet rather than speak courageously with grace and truth. We hurl curses rather than blessings. How can we use the gift of communication to love God and serve others well? How can we develop communication skills that will benefit us throughout our lives? Is it possible to unleash the power of communication to truly make a difference in this world? *Unwrapping the Gift of Communication* answers these questions; it offers practical ways for developing life-giving, other-centered, communication skills.

Jones reminds us that as Christ followers we are called to use the gift of communication to make others feel loved and valued. "Tell me what you hear me saying"—a phrase to check if we are communicating clearly. "Tell me more"—a phrase that says, I am listening. "Can you please help me understand why you feel that way?"—a question to address conflict productively. Jones shares specific phrases and questions to practice healthy ways of communicating—language we can use as we seek clarification, listen well, deal with conflicts, and much more.

Jones does not stop there. He assigns exercises to reinforce these productive ways of communicating. For example, the chapter on confirming messages, words that make other people feel valued, concludes with a challenge: Try to go one entire day without saying anything negative and then write a one-page journal entry about your experiences. Could you go an entire day without saying anything negative? I assigned this challenge to students in my interpersonal communication class. Here are two comments:

- "I realized that I can no longer allow a mindset of passive negativity to steal my joy. The first step in cultivating a genuine joy is to take control of my thought process."

- "It [the exercise] was helpful in the way that it made me far more aware of my words throughout the day; I hope that this experience sticks with me and causes me to think twice from now on and be more intentional with my words."

As I read through the journal entries, I heard students acknowledging how hard it is to stay positive, but also recognizing the importance of weighing words carefully before speaking. A great lesson learned. We all have so much to learn, and Jones is a wonderful teacher. Each chapter has these kinds of exercises to help us learn how to more faithfully tell others that they matter. Jones also clearly and engagingly introduces communication theories and then provides biblical examples of them.

"He [Jesus] poured water into a basin and began to wash his disciples' feet, drying them with the towel that was wrapped around him" (John 13:5). By washing the feet of his disciples, Jesus violates both the disciples' expectations of their Messiah as well as cultural expectations, showing that we need to prioritize our relationships over our norms—a scriptural illustration of Expectancy Violation Theory.

"'One thing you lack,' he [Jesus] said. 'Go sell everything you have and give to the poor and you will have treasure in heaven. Then come, follow me.'" At this the man's face fell. He went away sad because he had great wealth" (Mark 10: 21–22). The rich man thought the cost of following Jesus was too much to bear—a scriptural illustration of Social Exchange Theory.

"A man was going down from Jerusalem to Jericho when he was attacked by robbers. They stripped him of his clothes, beat him and went away, leaving him half dead. A priest happened to be going down the same road, and when he saw the man, he passed by on the other side. So too, a Levite, when he came to the place and saw him, passed by on the other side. But a Samaritan, as he traveled, came where the man was; and when he saw him, he took pity on him. He went to him and bandaged his wounds, pouring on oil and wine. Then he put the man on his own donkey, brought him to an inn and took care of him" (Luke 10: 30–34). The Samaritan faced a decision: keep walking or show compassion by helping the hurting—a scriptural illustration of Cognitive Dissonance Theory.

Jones does not just describe these theories. With plenty of practical applications and penetrating questions, he shows us how to apply these theories in our everyday lives: What expectations do you place on the people in your life? How do you respond when expectations are violated? When you first engaged in your relationship with God, what were your original perceptions of the cost to you versus the reward you were receiving? Did you ever experience Cognitive Dissonance with your faith? Piercing questions aren't they?

This book reminds us that it is only through God's grace that we can communicate in ways that serve others well. Each chapter ends with a prayer, expressing gratitude to our Heavenly Father for the gift of communication, and asking him to help us use this gift as he intended:

- "Father, thank you for your gift of communication."
- "Please help me remember to stop and ask myself, 'How is what I am about to say going to make the other person feel?'"
- "I pray for wisdom to know how to use words that will honor you."

Unwrapping the Gift of Communication is a gift to its readers. A gift to unwrap and to use. A gift, offering biblically informed, research-based strategies for communicating in ways that truly serve others and honor our Lord Jesus Christ. I cannot wait to use this gift in my courses. And I cannot wait to hear how others—whether students, church study groups, or individual Christians—benefit from the wisdom in this book.

Diane M. Badzinski, PhD
Chair, Professor of Communication, Colorado
Christian University
Co-author, *Family Communication and the Christian Faith: An Introduction and Exploration* (with Jonathan Pettigrew); *An Essential Guide to Interpersonal Communication: Building Great Relationships with Faith, Skill, and Virtue in the Age of Social Media* (with Quentin Schultze)

Introduction

Discovering the Gift of Communication

Seeing Clearly and 1 Corinthians 13:12

> An understanding of the principle of our own growth enables us
> to search out correct principles with the confidence that the more
> we learn, the more clearly we can focus the lens through which
> we see the world. The principles don't change; our understanding
> of them does.[1]
>
> —Stephen R. Covey

I HAVE BEEN BLESSED TO HAVE TRAVELED on many journeys to different
places in the world. Some of those journeys have been on my own or with
my wife and several journeys have involved taking students on educational
trips to faraway countries. Every journey has been an incredible adventure
to explore this world God created. Despite how great the adventures were,
some of the journeys were fraught with challenges, obstacles, or setbacks.
I have stepped off a plane in Peru only to discover my luggage is in El
Salvador, and no one has any idea what to do about it. I had a plane in
Africa take off eight hours late, only to land in a different country over
three thousand miles from where I was supposed to be lecturing. I had
crippling altitude sickness the first time I went to Machu Picchu. I spent
three days in a remote hospital in Ecuador after a bad mountain bike accident fractured my pelvic bone in three places. I got stuck in a torrential
downpour in a taxi at eleven o'clock at night in Havana, Cuba, convinced
I was going to die.

The list of challenges I have encountered on my adventures goes on
and on. However, no matter how stressful the obstacles on a trip (like that
mountain bike accident in Ecuador that resulted in an eight-hour ride
in the back of a jeep to the nearest hospital), my memories of the trips
do not dwell on the setbacks. My memories are filled with the wonderful

adventures I have been blessed to experience, the places I have seen, and the people I have met.

The experiences of my journeys around the world are like the writing of this book. This book has been a journey, filled with obstacles and challenges, some of which have been very hard and discouraging. But now that the final manuscript is done, I have forgotten most of the challenges, and dwell more on the potential of the finished product.

Like most books, moving from inception to completion is a very involved process. The journey of this book goes back some 30 years. The following are some of the pieces of that journey. Several years ago, the pastor of the church I was attending at the time asked me to speak to his staff about developing better listening skills. I eagerly combined what I taught in my communication studies classrooms with biblical support and shared it with the staff. It must have gone well because my pastor asked me to speak at our church's annual marriage retreat on how to explore healthy relational communication. I spent hours combing Scripture to find examples of some of the basic communication theories I was teaching and was able to prepare an entire weekend of material. I began speaking at other churches through word-of-mouth referrals and my world of theory came to life through Scripture.

At the time I was getting the chance to do all of this, I was teaching at a non-faith-based college. As a result, I was not able to take these newfound connections into my classroom. Through an unusual chain of events, I left the school I was teaching at and moved one thousand miles away to a faith-based private Christian college. The move also meant leaving the church where I had begun teaching about communication and relationships. As a result of now teaching at a faith-based college, I was able to begin connecting Scripture to communication topics and activities on a regular basis in the classroom. The more I read and re-read Scripture, the more I found all sorts of biblical ties to communication practices. My life took some unfortunate twists, and I became a single dad. Between my family responsibilities and my work responsibilities, my research on biblical examples of communication got put on hold for several years.

In the fall of 2017, I was asked to teach the senior capstone class for my Department of Communication Studies. As I prepared for the class, a wild idea popped into my head. I decided to see if this group of senior communication studies majors could share in my journey. I assigned the class a project requiring them to find biblical examples of the numerous communication theories the students had spent the past several years learning. To my delight, the students came up with several wonderful examples and ideas. Many of those ideas are in this book and those students are listed on my acknowledgment page.

It was from that class I got the idea for a book that would combine biblical truths with communication theories to help people navigate communication and relationships. I drafted many possible chapters and sent them to a variety of friends for feedback. Those drafts were not well received so I buried the idea and just continued to teach my communication courses and develop the ideas for my classes. As I revised and refined my ideas over the next several years, students began to give me some great feedback. When it came time for a sabbatical in the fall of 2022, I decided to commit my sabbatical to writing this book. This time, I did so under the guidance of the wonderful editors at Integratio Press.

As I began researching this topic, I found some faith-based communication books written by academics for the college classroom. One of the biggest takeaways I found in these works was the concept of communication being a gift from God. The ability to use words (language) to create meaning with other human beings is uniquely human. I explore this idea in greater detail in Chapter 1 of this book. As I shared this concept of communication being a gift from God with my students, they began asking me why this "gift" could cause so many problems in relationships. That was a great question I felt deserved an answer.

From my days of speaking at churches on communication, the Bible, and marriages, I knew that many couples struggled with the same question. If God gave them this gift, then why were their marriages struggling so much with communication problems? I was convicted that the next part of this journey needed to include searching for some answers to that question. As I talked with more and more couples about their communication challenges, I began to see a disconnect between God's word and how people used their gift. My research showed me that God gave us an owner's manual, his word, to help us navigate his gift of communication. The struggling couples that I talked to needed help figuring out how to use the owner's manual. That revelation led me to the conviction that I wanted to write a book that could be helpful in faith-based communication classrooms as well as used by couples, pastors, churches, and marriage counselors in a church. It is from that journey that this book emerged.

Writing for two different audiences is filled with challenges. The academic audience wants research and data to support all the claims being made. The church audience seems to prefer more practical tools on how to improve communication. Chapter 1 may read as heavy academic content, but the rest of the chapters work to find a clear balance between the two worlds. Regardless of what each audience wants, the needs are still the same—to understand how to have healthy communication in our daily relationships. This book is the culmination of my journey of many years of teaching communication and studying the Bible. Along the way, my journey has included becoming a single dad, remarrying, discovering the joys and challenges of a blended family, and several other unanticipated twists and turns. It is from this journey that I draw compassion and insight into what it means to be a flawed human trying to figure out how to use my "gift" of communication.

I have worn glasses for many years. I originally began wearing glasses because I had trouble seeing things far away and I needed glasses with lenses that clarified things that were in the distance. A few years ago, I discovered a new problem. I started having trouble seeing objects that were close such as books or my computer. A trip to the optometrist resulted in a pair of bi-focal glasses, glasses with two different lenses. My new glasses combined the lens I needed for seeing objects in the distance, with the lens I needed for up-close reading. My vision was very clear no matter what the circumstance. This book is written from the same perspective. I combine the lens of communication theory with the lens of biblical teachings to create a clearer vision of how to "see" God's gift. Each chapter highlights both lenses.

For each topic area, the "lens" of a communication theory is defined and explored to lay a foundation for the reader to understand how a particular communication tool or skill works. The "lens" of a biblical passage or verse is provided to illustrate how God was aware that his "gift" of communication would be fraught with challenges, so he gave people of faith an owner's manual on how to navigate any challenges the gift might bring. Those lenses are followed in each chapter with steps to take to unwrap the gift for everyday life. It is easy to become complacent and leave a gift packed away in a box if you do not know how to use it. My prayer for each reader is to provide you with enough information and skills so you can unwrap your gift and enjoy it. While humans use language to communicate, that does not guarantee that all language use is healthy and honors God's gift. With the lenses provided in this book, I pray that your language and communication become healthier and more honoring to God.

There is a distinct difference between when you see the world with a clear lens versus a poor or dirty lens. In Paul's first letter to the Corinthians, he used a similar metaphor for seeing things clearly when he wrote "We don't yet see things clearly. We're squinting in a fog, peering through a mist. But it won't be long before the weather clears, and the sun shines bright! We'll see it all then, see it all as clearly as God sees us, knowing him directly just as he knows us!" (13:12, The Message). God knew you needed a clear lens in the form of his owner's manual to help you see how to use his gift of language well. It is my hope that his book allows you to see your gift as clearly as I now see things both far away and up close with my new glasses.

There are many ways to study the gift of communication. Quentin Schultze, in his book, *Communicating with Grace and Virtue*, challenged followers of Jesus to realize that we do not have to be perfect communicators.[2] We just need to accept the call to communicate well. The author notes, "Communication is too important to take for granted. It is a gift from God that we can develop, enjoy, and use to serve others as we would like to be served. I call it *servant communication*."[3]

My desire is for every reader of this book is to allow each chapter to move you closer to the goal of servant communication. I would love to see your communication skills grow as you read each chapter, and from your growth, learn what it means to engage servanthood when you communicate. However, to grow, you must be willing to learn. In the Book of Proverbs, the author instructs people of faith to maintain teachable hearts: "A person who turns from correction faces poverty and shame, but one who regards constructive criticism is well respected" (13:18, Voice Translation). Nothing in this book matters if you are not willing to learn and explore how you can improve this very important topic in your life. In a relationship, both parties need to be willing to see ways that they can work together to improve communication rather than focusing on pointing fingers.

Growing in your knowledge of good communication skills can allow you to avoid the dangers of what has been named the *dark side of communication*.[4] Authors Tim Muehlhoff and Todd Lewis identified the dark side of communication to include, "Verbal abuse, sarcasm, hate speech, diatribes, humiliation, and ridicule."[5] The two-sided nature of communication is addressed in Proverbs when the writer noted, "Through the blessing of the upright a city is exalted, but by the mouth of the wicked it is destroyed" (11:11). The world of sinful humanity often provokes us to embrace the dark side of communication and to use it to hurt people. But

God planned and intended our gift to be used as a servant—to engage the gift in a way that honors God and builds relationships. As you read each chapter, you will find suggestions for ways to engage in servant communication as well as a prayer prompt to help you pray specifically for ways you can practice servant communication. It is my prayer these tools help you avoid the entrapments of the dark side of communication and embrace your gift for all it is worth.

As a professor of communication studies, I have been blessed by the opportunity to teach students many different communication theories. The more I teach these different theories and the more I read the Bible, the more I see the connection between the two. I love to point out how modern theories are finally catching up to what God already provided in Scripture many years ago.

The purpose of this book is to unwrap our gift of communication through both the lens of Scripture and the lens of communication theories. By combining these lenses, the reader has a 3D vision or greater depth perception to unwrap the gift. The application of Scripture will be followed by an explanation of how you can apply the theory in your everyday relational communication. Questions such as, "What have you learned from this application," and, "How does it affect your life as a person of faith?" will be explored. Each chapter will provide steps you can apply to your life along with a prayer prompt you can use to cover and protect your communication skills. A set of follow-up questions that can be used for classroom discussions or assignments, or small group Bible studies, are provided at the end of each chapter.

As I explore the role of Scripture, I refer to myself and other Christ followers as "people of faith." Years ago, I felt the word "Christian" had acquired too much negative baggage in our culture. I began calling myself a person of faith for several reasons. My belief in God, the provision of his Son for salvation, my daily walk through life, and what should drive every decision I make, is my faith. Calling myself a person of faith reminds me daily of those convictions and beliefs. Also, years ago I learned that to be "a person of faith" I had to live by that faith in all aspects of my life. Using that title reminds me that I am called in 2 Corinthians to "Walk by faith, and not by sight" (5:7, KJV). When the challenges of life overwhelm me, calling myself a person of faith convicts me that I am called to walk by that faith.

While this book is part of my journey on this topic, it is far from the end of my journey. I still have much more to learn. My prayer is that the words in this book can be a valuable part of your journey—no matter what the stage of your journey or the obstacles you encounter along the way. Some of the material in this book may not apply to every reader, but I believe that there are some ideas and tools in this book that every reader can find useful in some way. This book cannot provide you with all the answers you need, but I believe it includes many answers to help you navigate your journey with your gift of communication. I wish you a wonderful adventure as you read this book.

Chapter 1

Where Did We Get This Gift?

The Wonder of Human Communication and Psalm 139:14

Perhaps the gift you seek, already resides within you, awaiting the day you choose to unwrap it.[1]

—Truth Devour

PSALM 139:14 RECOGNIZED what remarkable creations human beings are by declaring, "I praise you for I am fearfully and wonderfully made." The word "fearfully" does not mean afraid or scared but is translated as "to revere or be in reverence" as if the writer was "in awe or wonderment."[2] The Psalmist looked at the design of the human body and could only stand before God in awe and praise. In fact, the human brain is so incredible that replicating its functions continues to be one of the biggest challenges for robotics.

Among the many incredible capabilities of the human body is the ability to engage in language. All animals can communicate in some manner or form, but only human beings communicate with language. Linguist Noam Chomsky posited that humans are "wired" to develop language.[3] Chomsky's declaration provoked many questions, among them, "Why do only humans have language?"[4] After Charles Darwin published, *On the Origin of Species*, many scholars turned to evolution for an explanation of human language acquisition and found none.[5] It was determined that the origins of language simply could not be explained by the theory of natural selection.[6] Moreover, other species evidently lack the ability to acquire language. A challenge was given in Darwin's time that no one could raise and train apes to speak with language.[7] Since that challenge was made, many researchers have tried. In 1933, one couple attempted to raise a chimpanzee alongside their son. The chimpanzee did not acquire language and, in fact, the chimpanzee's influence hindered the son's development. After nine months, the experiment was abandoned. The conclusion of the study was that apes do not have the vocal apparatus to imitate human sounds.[8]

Recent studies have arrived at similar results but yielded stronger conclusions.[9] In the 1970s, one couple raised a chimpanzee named Washoe with their infant children. Washoe was also unable to learn language.[10] The Washoe study was followed by an extended study of animal language acquisition at Columbia University with a chimpanzee named Nim (The chimpanzee's full name was Neam "Nim" Chimpsky, a direct pun on Chomsky's name with the intent of proving Chomsky wrong). Nim was the first female chimpanzee to learn sign language, but researchers eventually concluded that Nim merely used random gestures until receiving a reward, and then learned to mimic symbols of American Sign Language from her teachers to get a reward: she did not actually understand the language, nor could she create sentences. The leader of the project, Herbert Terrace, concluded, "Objective analysis of our data, as well as those obtained by other studies, yielded no evidence of an ape's ability to use grammar."[11] Terrace later published a work titled *Why Chimpanzees Can't Learn Language and Only Humans Can.*[12] Following these conclusions, researchers turned to a comparative method,[13] identifying humans' and other primates' various components of communication and then making cross-species comparisons for each component.[14] The research resulted in the same conclusion about language: Humans have it, and other species do not.[15]

This is not to say that other species do not communicate. They clearly do. But their communication takes a much different form, using a type of "Code Model"[16] or fixed set of signals, for the transmission of information from one animal to another.[17] Code Models depend upon simple associations of one sort or another, mostly determined by instinct, which together make up an animal's world of meaning.[18] These predetermined associations are much more limited than the meanings experienced by humans. For instance, when animal researchers use the term "meaning," they typically mean a command or directive to which other animals will instinctively or habitually respond. When a dog growls and barks, the message is clear to all recipients—stay away. The "waggle dance" which honeybees use to indicate the location of sources of nectar involves a combination of distinct elements. The direction the bee faces during the main part of the dance indicates the direction of the nectar, and the duration of the dance indicates the distance to the nectar.[19] When an animal produces a mating call, the meaning is "come mate with me."[20] The code that was sent corresponds to the exact message that was received.

With human language, however, there is a wide range of meaning beyond just simple commands or objects, and this creates a potential for misunderstanding. If I were to say "I love you" to a person, that statement could mean many different things. The reason for this is language consists of symbols rather than signal codes. Scholars have determined that the biggest difference between animal codes and human language revolves around the difference between signs and symbols.[21] A sign is "Anything that announces the existence or the imminence of some event, the presence or a thing or person, or a change in the state of affairs."[22] In contrast, a symbol brings something to mind and causes a person to think about the thing symbolized in diverse and potentially creative ways.[23] In this way, it allows us to reflect on things that may or may not be present in our environment and choose a response. While animal "signs" and human "symbols" both involve a mode of communication, semanticity (meaning), and pragmatic function (useful purpose),[24] the symbol system of human language also includes two distinctive features: "displacement" (the ability to communicate about things that are not present in space or time) and "productivity" (the ability to produce and understand any number of messages that have never been expressed before and may express novel ideas).[25] As a result, human language is an open system and animal communication is a closed system. Animal codes mean exactly what the code was intended to mean, while human symbols can have numerous meanings. To date, no animal communication system has been identified that meets all the criteria of human symbols.[26]

In addition to communicating through symbol systems, only humans use what is called Ostensive-Inferential Communication: the expression and recognition of communicative intentions.[27] This expression and recognition is achieved by the proactive use of evidence: signalers provide evidence for their intentions, and receivers interpret it. This means that to construct appropriate signals, (in this case, messages composed of symbols), signalers must consider not just what it is they wish to communicate, but also their knowledge and beliefs about what their audience already knows or believes, given the current context. Receivers must do something similar, but in reverse: they must consider not just the form that the signal takes, but also the context and their knowledge and beliefs about the signaler's general motivations and intentions.[28] This is how saying, "I *love* my wife" has an entirely different meaning from when I say, "I *love* the color of that flower." All of this shows that the creation, development, and use of language requires a cognitive process for the signaler and signaled to reason their way through a message. Scholars have acknowledged that there is a clear difference in the cognitive abilities required for Ostensive-Inferential Communication, and those required for the Code Models of all other animals.

In addition to the higher cognitive capacity required to communicate through language, many biological differences give humans the ability to use language. The biological foundations of human language are many and they enable such things as speech production, speech perception, language processing, memory, and imitation. For example, the design of the human body gives humans the ability to produce highly sophisticated repertoires of sounds used in language. In primate species, and indeed, most mammals, the larynx, which houses the vocal folds that manipulate the pitch and volume of vocalization, sits high in the throat. However, in adult humans it is descended; it sits lower in the throat. A descended larynx makes it possible for humans to produce a far greater range of speech sounds than would otherwise be possible.[29] Another example of a human's distinctive physical capacity for language was found in the 2003 report of the Genome Project, a decade-long study of DNA. Scientists studied human DNA and animal DNA and found that among the differences between human beings and animals was the presence of a gene for hearing acuity which is found only in humans.[30] Hearing acuity is the ability to detect minute differences in sound which play a large role in learning, hearing, and interpreting language.

Humans' distinctive capacity for language goes hand in hand with free will and an ethical responsibility as God's image bearers. Symbols are necessary for choice to exist. If every communication symbol a human used had a fixed meaning like animal codes, then humans would lose the ability to make and have choices. However, symbols are open-ended, enabling reflection and creativity. This free will component of symbols creates a responsibility to consider how others might interpret messages. Humans have the freedom to choose a symbol and use it in a way that honors God's gift. However, being human means sometimes making poor choices with our gift.

While it is easy to marvel at how our bodies are wonderfully made and praise God for sight, hearing, a beating heart, or childbirth, giving thanks to the Lord for the gift of communication may not quickly come to mind. Yet, as we have seen, our human capacity to use language to create meaning is extremely complex and requires a combination of cognitive and physical capacities that no other animals share. Language allows us to make conscious choices, to create, to infer what others are thinking, and to interpret their messages. In short, it is language that allows us to do some of the things that God does. But if being human is to be made in the likeness of God, and the ability to create language is an essential part of that likeness, then why is good, healthy communication with other people sometimes so challenging? I would argue that the challenge comes from how easy it is to take our gift of communication for granted. We fail to "unwrap" God's gift by studying the "owner's manual"—the Bible—to understand how to use our gift well. We have the freedom to choose our words and sometimes we make poor choices. It is sometimes too easy saying the first words that pop into our minds rather than exercising self-control and thinking before we speak.

Given the awesome complexity of human language, I begin most of my communication courses with a discussion of how our gift of language, and thus communication, is crucial to being made in God's likeness. I show students how God has wonderfully created us with this gift. I then tell my students that for the rest of the semester, we are going to explore how to better understand this gift we have been given and why the world is so focused on hiring good, effective communicators.[31] The world wants people who are living out the likeness of God. I also share with each class how my life is far from perfect, and how I have made many, many communication errors in my life (and still do). Just because I teach this topic does not mean I have discovered a magic formula for perfect communication. I have discovered, however, that God knew the gift would bring challenges. That is why God provided some tools in Scripture to help you navigate your gift, as well as endowing humans with the capacity to scientifically examine how communication works. The goal of this book is to provide each reader with some insights from Scripture and communication theory that I have discovered in my 35-plus years of teaching on how to better communicate in everyday interactions and relationships.

5 Ways to Unwrap Your Gift of Communication

1. Try to remember how incredible and special God's gift of language is for you. God created you with the tools needed to use language and create meaning. Humans are the only animal on this planet that have this ability to create meaning. Whenever possible, try to remember to give a quick prayer of thanks to God for his gift.

2. Remind yourself that communication is a complicated gift that by design can, unfortunately, be fraught with problems. That is normal and part of being human. Commit to investing in applying the material found in the rest of this book to develop better communication skills.

3. What are some ways you have allowed a breakdown in communication to hinder or harm a relationship? Are these communication challenges a regular part of everyday life or once-in-a-while rare encounters? If the challenges happen more often than you would prefer, commit to being open to what the following chapters in this book have to offer you for ways to address those challenges.

4. Forgive yourself for the times you have misused your gift of communication. God knew his gift would create challenges, which is why he gave us an owner's manual. It is OK to make mistakes as long as you actively try to learn from those mistakes and do your best to not repeat the mistake.

5. Ask God to forgive you for any time you have misused his gift. God promised us that "If we confess our sins, He is faithful to forgive us our sins."[32] After receiving forgiveness, commit to more fully unwrapping your gift so you honor God with how you use your gift.

We have a family member who is notorious for the way they save Christmas wrapping paper. Every gift they receive on Christmas morning is slowly and carefully opened so the wrapping paper is not torn. You may have a family member who does the same thing. They then fold each piece of paper to be saved and re-purposed someday. They do the same thing with the ribbons and bows. Growing up with my parents who survived the Great Depression, I understand the "everything must be reused" mentality. Unfortunately, our children function more from a young, impulsive, "get-the-gift-opened" mentality. Ripping the paper to shreds to get to the gift is their top priority. The family member's approach to gift opening can drive them crazy. When the children ask why they take so long, rather than give a long story about the need to repurpose, they merely reply, "These gifts are from all of you and each one is precious to me just like you are precious to me. I don't want to open the gift in any way that might damage it."

My prayer for you is that by the end of this book, you not only see the value of unwrapping your gift of communication with care, but you understand how precious the gift is. This gift can bring great joy and fulfillment and this gift can bring great hurt and pain. If you rip open your gift and quickly discard the wrapping like my children on Christmas morning, you risk missing out on how precious the gift can be. But if you take your time, carefully read this book, remain open to ideas that might be uncomfortable at first but can be grounded in Scripture, and make an honest effort to apply the application steps to your life, you have the chance to see how precious the gift can be and not miss out on why the gift was given to you in the first place.

• Prayer Prompt •

Father, thank you for your gift of communication. Please forgive me for ways I may have misused your gift, hurt others with my words, not listened in love, and not honored you with my communication. I ask for help from the Holy Spirit with my words so I can show your love to others with the words I speak. I ask for wisdom to pause before I speak and use my gift for you. As I read this book, please open my eyes and heart to ideas on ways I can improve my communication skills. Thank you for this opportunity to better understand this gift you have given me. In Jesus's name, Amen.

Chapter 1: Follow-Up Questions

1. How does the argument about human DNA and human beings being the only animal on the planet to use language strike you? Is it hard to believe or does it offer you some insight into the challenges of communication?

2. The author described some communication challenges as a failure to unwrap the gift of communication God gave you. How does that argument strike you? Do you agree or disagree? Why or why not?

3. What questions does this introduction raise for you (if any)?

4. Based on the overview of the book in the introduction and Chapter 1, is there something you are looking forward to as you read each chapter?

5. Have you ever (intentionally or unintentionally) ripped open the wrapping paper on your gift of communication and misused it? What happened and what might be some ways you could more slowly unwrap your gift next time?

Chapter 2

Understanding How the Gift of Communication Works

The Six Elements of All Messages and James 1:19

Once a human being has arrived on this earth, communication is the largest single factor determining what kinds of relationships she or he makes with others and what happens to each in the world. How we manage survival, how we develop intimacy, how productive we are, how we make sense, how we connect with our own divinity—all depend largely on our communication skills.[1]

—Virginia Satir

But the most notable and profitable invention of all others, was that of communication. . . whereby humans register their thoughts; recall them when they are past; and also declare them one to another.[2]

—Thomas Hobbes

SEVERAL YEARS AGO, MY FAMILY WAS ON VACATION, and we went to a local restaurant for dinner. The restaurant was loud and lively with music and a DJ. At one point during our meal, the DJ announced a dance contest to a popular song at the time that had specific dance moves. The DJ announced, "The best dancer to this song will get free shots!" Our 15-year-old daughter jumped up and said, "I know this dance!" and ran off to the dance floor to compete before we could stop her. My wife and I thought that the DJ would remove a minor from the contest given the announced prize, so we let her dance. Well, to our dismay, not only was she allowed to dance, but she won the dance contest. A waitress came up to her with a tray of shot glasses full of tequila and announced, "Here are your *shots!*" Before we could step in and stop everything, our daughter responded in disgust, "*Shots*?? I thought the DJ said '*socks!*' I wanted to win a pair of *socks!*"

Our daughter walked away terribly disappointed, and fortunately, we did not have to intervene and stop the consumption of the prize. (And to be honest, to this day my wife and I have never figured out why a free pair of socks was so exciting to win.) But what a difference one word can make. One person said "*shots,*" but another person heard "*socks.*" It is amazing how just one word can change an entire message. Perhaps you have experienced miscommunication like this due to a missed word, a misinterpreted word, or zoning out during a conversation and missing an entire sentence or two. It can truly change the entire conversation, and often not for the better. Unfortunately, miscommunication like this is not unusual. In fact, it happens all the time and often without any ill intent. The DJ clearly and honestly said "shots," but our daughter clearly believed she heard and interpreted the message as "socks." How does this happen or even more importantly, why does this happen and how do we respond when it does happen? This chapter will explore the nature of messages to provide some insight into how and why miscommunication can happen so easily, explore how Scripture helps us navigate this problem, and review some steps we can follow to avoid miscommunication as much as possible.

The Six Elements of the Communication Process[3]

To better understand how communication works, it is important to use the communication process lens. All messages involve six different elements of the communication process, three on the part of the sender and three on the part of the receiver. These elements are listed below in the sequence they logically follow (almost like "stages" in communication), but because both parties in a conversation are proactively engaged in making meaning, they do not always occur in sequential order. For example, a receiver may anticipate or assume what the sender will say and respond accordingly (verbally or nonverbally) before the sender has spoken; and this response may affect what the sender will actually say. Thus, the elements can jump around, overlap, backtrack, or even flow from one to the other smoothly. Every conversation is different, so every unwrapping of the elements will be different.

Receiver	Sender
1. What the sender wants to say.	4. What the receiver hears.
2. What the sender does say.	5. How the receiver interprets what they think they heard.
3. How the sender says what they want to say.	6. How the receiver responds to what they interpreted.

The first element of a message is, "What the sender wants to say," otherwise known as the original thought in the sender's mind. The thought can be well formulated, partially prepared, or made up on the spot. Whatever the origin, the thought is the original idea. However, what you prepare to say and what comes out of your mouth are sometimes not the same. This brings us to the second element, "What the sender does say." There are times when what we say gets jumbled and our tongue gets tied up for no reason. It just happens. If our thoughts are not well prepared or formulated, we say the first thing that comes to our minds, which may not be the best thing. I have often wanted to grab my words out of the air and shove them back into my mouth as soon as I say them.

There are times when you cannot share the exact thought in your mind because you are not sure the audience can or should hear it. You must translate your thoughts to be more appropriate. That translation can cause a breakdown in communication. For example, a few years ago, one of our family members became very sick. When my (then) 20-year-old daughter asked the age-old question, "Why does God let bad things happen to good people?" it was appropriate to share what I *wanted* to say. I discussed with her God's providence, free will, and many other adult topics. However, when my (then) 10-year-old son asked, "Why did God let Grandpa get sick?" I had to change what I *wanted* to say so my son could process the information better. The message was changed and may have gotten lost in the translation. If you do not know how to rephrase or change a message to adapt to your audience, you can find yourself miscommunicating or unintentionally upsetting your audience.

While the first two elements of the communication process can cause plenty of challenges to a communicator, every message contains additional elements. There is a third element of the communication process that can complicate things even more. It is one thing to have what you wanted to say, and then what you did say, but it is also important to understand the third element: "How the sender says what they want to say." Vocal tone, inflection, rate of speech, use of pauses, and many other forms of non-verbal communication can change the entire message being sent. This element of communication may even be a part of the previous elements. You can choose how you want to deliver your words at the same time you are formulating the words in your mind. One sentence can be said in two entirely different ways to communicate entirely different meanings. The statement, "Kevin, he's a *great* guy," means one thing when the emphasis is placed on the word "great." But if the emphasis changes to, "Kevin? *He's* a great guy" (with a sarcastic tone on "great guy"), the same sentence has an entirely different meaning.

With each sender element comes the opportunity for a communication breakdown. By the time the sender speaks (or texts, direct messages, etc.), element one and element three can turn out to be two entirely different messages. Yet, the communication process does not end there; the receiver filters the message through three more elements.

In the fourth element of the communication process, the receiver hears the words. This element of communication requires the receiver to perceive the message and retranslate it into an idea.[4] The listener is doing the same thing as the sender, but in reverse. This requires both sender and receiver to have similar worlds of meaning. The chances of the sender and receiver having the exact shared worlds of meaning is very small. Therefore, the opportunities for miscommunication are very high. Additionally, rarely is just the sender sending or just the receiver receiving. Both parties are sending and receiving simultaneously. This simultaneous transaction further increases the chance for miscommunication as words are missed or misunderstood and each person is reacting to the other person's misinterpreted words.

Maybe you have heard someone say something to you, but like my daughter and the restaurant DJ, you missed one or two words due to competing noise or a quick mental lapse. You think the missed words do not matter only to find out later that you missed a major part of the message. You can also jumble the message due to your filters or how you attach meaning to messages. When you hear words, you place them into an order that makes sense for you. This involves a person's world of meaning.[5] When you hear a message, you naturally listen for familiar categories, trying to fit data into your existing schemata. It is very hard to avoid doing this. If you can catch yourself doing this, you can try to be aware of what you are doing and check with the sender that you are understanding the sent message correctly. Part of the challenge is that the sending of a message and your quick interpretation or categorizing of information can all happen quickly and simultaneously. We must pay attention to what we hear.

Our filters also directly affect our reaction to a message. If you were raised in a home where sarcasm was never allowed and you were even told that sarcasm was not appropriate communication for people of faith, then if I deliver a sarcastic message to you, and even mean it completely in jest, you will be unable to receive it that way. You may even pass judgment and cut off communication with me without ever finding out what I meant by my message.

The fifth element of communication (also known as the second element on the receiver side), is "How the receiver interprets what they think they heard." The receiver of the message hears words, sentences, nouns, verbs, vocal inflection, vocal tone, and many other parts of the message. You naturally organize what you hear so you can make sense of the message and understand what is being said. However, it is easy to misinterpret what you think you heard, (e.g., shots versus socks). I am sure you can recall a time when you interpreted a message from a person one way and responded to that interpretation only to find out you completely misinterpreted the message. It has happened to just about everyone. One of my daughters does not read sarcasm well and I have often said something to her with a statement that was, in my mind, a sarcastic joke only to have her respond in anger and hurt. She interpreted my sarcastic tones as a critical indictment of her. I have had to learn to change "what I want to say" and "what I actually say" with my daughter because of how she interprets messages.

How you interpret a message has a direct effect on the sixth and final element of communication, "How the receiver responds to what they interpreted." If the receiver misinterprets the message, then there is a large probability that the response is going to be inappropriate. The receiver should make sure they have the clearest possible interpretation of the message possible, then their response can be appropriate for the communication process to proceed on a positive and clear route. However, if the receiver has misinterpreted the message and responds inappropriately then the communication process will probably proceed in a negative direction.

In any communication transaction, the goal is to get the original words in element one and the response to those words in element six to be as consistent as possible. Many times, this happens when both communicators work together to understand their responsibility and their role in the communication process. Communication is a two-way process, which means both the sender and receiver are sending and receiving messages simultaneously. When I speak to my daughter in a sarcastic tone, and she responds defensively, we are both responsible for the negative communication transaction. When she sends a defensive message, I read her message and see that it does not match what I intended to send. Rather than respond negatively, I can acknowledge her defensiveness and attempt to redirect the message.

Unwrapping the Elements of the Communication Process

There are three valuable lessons that can be learned from the six elements of communication. First, the only message that counts is the message received. Why? Because that is the message the receiver will respond to. It does not matter what you *meant* to say, or *wanted* to say, what matters is how the receiver interpreted the message because the message they are going to respond to sets off the next stage of the model. If I am not careful, I can quickly tell my daughter, "That is not what I meant" when she interpreted my sarcasm as criticism and then blame her for the entire breakdown in communication. Instead, I need to work with or from her interpretation of my message since that is how she framed it in her mind. As the elements of communication ebb and flow the opportunities for challenges are numerous. Rather than focus on what was misinterpreted, if I listen to her interpretation and respond to that message, then I can work to try and get it back on track.

A second valuable lesson to be learned from these elements of communication is to make sure that you have interpreted a message correctly before you respond to it. It is easy to misinterpret a message and react emotionally, which can take the communication transaction off in a completely different and possibly wrong direction. For example, my daughter has learned to ask, "Dad, are you being sarcastic or are you being serious?" She checks her interpretation before she responds to make sure she has interpreted my message correctly. This allows us to keep our conversation on track.

I often describe communication transactions to be like the old launches of the space shuttle. Everything about the launches of the shuttle had to be perfect. The shuttle could not take off if there was a chance it would not be on target. Leaving the earth just a few degrees off target could result in the shuttle ending up hundreds of miles off course when it reaches space. The launch plan was to go to point A, but the shuttle would end up at point B.

Sometimes conversations can be like the space shuttle. If a message (even one word) is misinterpreted in even the smallest way, the conversation can veer off course and the people speaking to one another can find themselves going in opposite directions. This can cause two communicators to have two completely different conversations. Perhaps you have experienced this phenomenon. Have you ever found yourself in the middle of a conversation realizing that you and the other person are having two completely different conversations? Maybe during the early stages of your communication exchange, one or both of you misinterpreted a word or two and the conversation strayed off track and went in different directions. After a few cycles of the stages of the communication process, your original message got so far off track it seemed hopeless. You may even feel like you and the other person just cannot communicate, when the truth is, you both just need to back up the conversation to see where the misinterpretation happened, and the message got off track.

One of the most important tools of communication you can learn is to make sure you have interpreted the message accurately before you respond. How can you do this? By simply asking questions. My daughter asks me to clarify my message before she responds, and it saves us time not having a conversation that goes in the wrong direction. When you hear a message and you are not 100% sure what the sender meant, tell them your interpretation of the message, and ask them if your interpretation is correct. If my wife tells me, "Are you really wearing that shirt to church?" I can interpret it as criticism and respond defensively saying, "I like this shirt, stop criticizing what I wear." Or I can ask her, "Is there something wrong with it?" She then points out the two large holes in the shirt and I can respond from a place of understanding the intended message and agree that I probably should not wear a shirt to church with holes in it.

The third and perhaps the most valuable lesson we can learn from the six elements of communication is that we can identify where the breakdown in communication takes place. Some people might say it is the sender, other people might say it is the receiver. What these six elements of communication teach is that sometimes when there is a communication breakdown, it is nobody's fault. It just happens. Look back at the six stages listed above. A breakdown can happen at any one of the stages, between several of the stages, or at every stage. There are ample opportunities for communication to break down even in the simplest of conversations.

It can be hard to accept that communication can sometimes be nobody's fault because we love to play the blame game. It is easy to think, "If there is a communication problem, it certainly can't be me, so it has to be you." We make selfish claims such as, "If you would communicate more clearly, we would get along just fine" or "If you would just listen better, then we would communicate better." Sometimes, the communication breakdown can be the fault of the sender or the receiver. The sender could be very unclear with what he or she is saying, or the receiver could be making very little effort to listen and respond well. But that is not the case every time. Many times, it is nobody's fault. Often, my wife and I will be struggling with a conversation, and I can say, "I think we are having two different conversations; can we back up a second?" By stepping back to look at the conversation through the lens of the six elements, we skip the blame game, accept that communication breakdown happens, and work together to get back on track.

Why is it so tempting to play the blame game? I would call it pride. It is easy to think, "I must be right, so I blame you for the problem." Scripture is filled with warnings about the dangers and perils of our pride. In Proverbs 6:16–19, we are informed of seven things that God hates, with the first thing on the list being pride.[6] When you experience a breakdown in communication, check your pride at the door and consider, maybe it is nobody's fault.

James 1:19 and Navigating the Six Elements of Communication

The Book of James provides a great biblical lens for understanding how communication can so easily break down. The author was aware of the importance of asking questions before responding to a message in a possibly incorrect manner. As James says, "My dear brothers and sisters, take note of this: Everyone should be quick to listen, slow to speak and slow to become angry" (1:19). James admonished his readers to listen. That means paying attention to every word a person is saying. If a particular word or phrase is problematic for you, rather than get angry and lash out, you are told to be slow to speak. James did not write, "Say nothing at all." Instead, as seen through the lens of communication theory, by using the phrase "slow to speak," James is encouraging you to ask questions. Before you respond to the message you heard, make sure you heard the message accurately and are responding appropriately. When you lash out in anger at an incorrect message, you could be misusing your gift of communication. A better use of your gift of communication would be to seek clarification, like when my daughter hears a sarcastic message from me and asks what I meant by that statement rather than lashing out. When I explain what I meant, she can respond appropriately to the message. Her gift of communication is used in a way that honors the Giver of the gift.

5 Ways to Unwrap the Elements of Communication

1. Be slow to speak. There are many ways to do this, but one easy way to do this is by simply asking questions. Another way might involve taking a time-out to reflect on what the other person said before responding. James encouraged you to avoid speaking in anger. That is hard to do, especially if you have misinterpreted the message.

2. Pray for your communication. Ask God for wisdom to listen and the strength to ask questions and not respond in anger.

3. Remember the first three elements all messages go through—the sender's part of the transaction—and accept responsibility for your role in the process. Are you working hard to make sure that "What you want to say" and "What you do say" are on the same page as much as possible? If you are stuck on how to say what you want to say, admit it to the receiver. Tell them, "I am struggling and cannot find the words right now."

4. Remember the last three elements all messages go through—the receiver's part of the transaction—and accept your responsibility for your role in the process. Do you only hear the words and react to them without clarifying if your interpretation was accurate? Ask questions to make sure that what you are hearing and interpreting are on target, then respond to an accurate message.

5. Stop playing the blame game. It never does anyone any good to play this game. Realize that sometimes the breakdown in communication is really nobody's fault and do not spend so much energy pointing fingers. Miscommunication just happens sometimes due to the process of communication. Free yourself of that burden to need to blame someone.

Conclusion

Communication is a gift from God, but it is a complicated gift. This complexity can be a source of many challenges in your relationships. You may have even experienced the pain of a severed or terminated relationship because of a communication problem. We have been made in the image of God to be relational beings, but our relationships depend on communication to survive and grow.

When my daughter thought she was in a contest to win a free pair of socks, the DJ said "shots." As the DJ had no intention of deceiving or misleading anyone, so too can our daily communication break down without malice. Miscommunication just happens. By understanding the six elements of the message process, you can better understand how to back up a conversation and make sure that what a sender wants to say is what the receiver is responding to. You can be "quick to listen, slow to speak, and slow to become angry." This clearly honors God, the Giver of our gift who intended your communication to be a relationship-building tool, not a relationship destroyer.

• Prayer Prompt •

Father, thank you for your gift of communication. Thank you for giving me so much ability to control how I use your gift. Forgive me when I have responded too quickly to a message and caused miscommunication. Forgive me for not listening when someone has spoken to me, and forgive me when I have chosen the blame game to deflect responsibility for my role in the message. Help me remember the six elements of communication and give me the wisdom to know when to ask questions and not jump to conclusions based on the message I thought I heard. In Jesus's name, Amen.

Chapter 2: Follow-Up Questions

1. Which of the six elements of the communication process is the hardest for you to navigate well? Why?

2. Think of a recent communication problem you had with someone.

Can you identify where in the six elements the problem may have originated? What happened and how did it turn out?

3. Do you often ask questions to clarify your interpretation of a message before you respond? Is this something you could work on? How might you do that?

4. Do you ever play the blame game? Why do you think you want to blame someone else for a communication problem?

Chapter 3

Mirror, Mirror on the Wall

Self-Concept, Reflected Appraisal, and Matthew 9:20–22

Dear Lord, please let me be the person my dog thinks I am!
—Bumper Sticker

WHEN I WAS A CHILD, a traveling carnival would come to a local shopping center every year. Among the many rides and games available was the House of Mirrors. Perhaps you have seen or experienced one of these types of attractions. As my friends and I would walk through the House, the mirrors would be placed in a pattern that would make it difficult to figure out how to navigate the path due to the different reflections. Among the many mirrors creating havoc in the house were ones that would create a distorted picture of the viewer. The mirrors would make a person look very tall and thin, very short and stout, or even twisted. The distorted images of our bodies were always good for laughs and finger-pointing at each other's funny body shapes.

Sometimes people act as mirrors in your daily life: people can give you a distorted image of yourself like a carnival mirror. A person may look at you funny, react to something you say, or make a critical statement that is hurtful to you. Due to the negative message you received, you might think of yourself as inferior. This is especially true when the mirrored reflection comes from someone whose opinion of you matters a great deal. All too often you can let the way you think how other people see you affect how you see yourself. This phenomenon is called "reflected appraisal." The process of reflected appraisal can sometimes be positive and supportive, but sometimes it can be very distorted and give you an inaccurate perception of who you are. The reflection can either build you up or tear you down. It can make you feel loved and accepted or rejected and unloved. This chapter will look at how reflected appraisal affects your self-concept, how Scripture can help you navigate your self-perception, and some ways you can improve your perception of yourself.

Reflected Appraisal

According to Symbolic Interaction Theory, your self-concept, to some extent, is a result of reflected appraisal: a mirroring of others' judgments.[1] You see yourself the way you think other people see you. It is like looking into a mirror: when you see your reflection, you get an image or idea of what you look like. When someone whose opinion of you matters a great deal to you (such as a parent, a significant other, or a teacher), says or does something that communicates how they see you, you tend to see their apparent perception of you as your "reflection." This, in turn, causes you to see yourself the way you think other people see you. When you receive supportive messages, you learn to value and appreciate yourself.[2] When you receive critical signals or negative messages about yourself, you may feel less valued, less loved, or less capable.[3] Your self-concept reflects the messages you have received throughout your life—both in person and through social media.[4]

When you receive positive and supportive messages, you tend to believe that the other person sees you that way. A child raised in a home where they were praised for their strengths and character will grow to see themselves as strong and a person of good character. If a young boy cries when injured and is hugged by his parent, he feels loved and accepted for expressing his emotions. He can grow up to see the expression of emotions as a strength. If a young girl is praised by important people for her heart and character, regardless of what her body looks like, she can grow up to be a strong, confident woman.

The reverse is also true. If you receive negative or unsupportive messages from a person you care about, your self-perception will tend to reflect that appraisal, thus shaping a negative image of yourself. A child raised in a home where they are called stupid or useless will grow up to see themselves as stupid or useless. A young girl growing up in a home where she is told to "watch her figure" or "haven't you had enough to eat today" will see herself as overweight, feel unaccepted, and often develop body image issues that can lead to eating disorders. If a young boy cries when he gets injured but is told to "be tough, be a man, don't cry," then that boy may see himself as weak or inferior for expressing emotions and may grow up to see himself as an inferior person every time he feels an emotion.

The concept of reflected appraisal brings the importance of affirming communication into clear focus. Just as carnival mirrors distort your image and make you look physically flawed, others' disparaging words can cause you to see yourself as a flawed person. On the flip side, just as a good mirror can reflect how good your hair looks, so too can others' positive, affirming words about you cause you to see yourself as the wonderful creation God made.

Matthew 9:20–22 and Reflected Appraisal

The biblical lens of Matthew 9:20–22 provides a beautiful example of how a woman did not let poor reflected appraisal keep her from being loved by Jesus. In fact, she received a new appraisal for herself in the process of being healed from a 12-year disease. As Scripture tells the story:

> Just then a woman who had been subject to bleeding for twelve years came up behind him and touched the edge of his cloak. She said to herself, "If I only touch his cloak, I will be healed." Jesus turned and saw her. "Take heart, daughter," he said, "your faith has healed you." And the woman was healed at that moment.

The woman carried her disease for 12 years. We are not told what the disease was specifically, but the word used for bleeding in Greek means "to flow blood"[5] and implies that it was menstrual-related. In the Hebrew culture, the Old Testament associated menstruation not only with physical impurity, but with moral impurity and sin.[6] As a result, the Hebrew word for menstruation, *nidda*, came to refer not just to the menstrual discharge but to the menstruant herself. She too was discharged and excluded from her society by being banished to and quarantined in separate quarters.[7] If this woman's bleeding was menstrual, I can only imagine the rejection and hurtful appraisal she experienced. Her self-concept and self-worth had to have taken some hits. Her behavior indicates that she did not see herself as worthy enough to even talk to Jesus, let alone stop and ask him for healing. Her own self-appraisal reflected the critical appraisal that the world had thrown at her. The world continually screamed at her, "You are diseased, you are flawed, you are immoral, impure, sinful, and you are not worthy!"

In the face of such negativity, what faith this woman demonstrated.

Despite the messages from the world, she knew that by just touching Jesus's robe, he would heal her. Not only was she healed the instant she touched his robe, but Jesus stopped and offered his own "appraisal" of her. Jesus began with a term of loving endearment—daughter. He took compassion on her and told her she was worthy enough to be his daughter, despite how the world rejected her. Jesus then gave her more words of love and acceptance, "Take heart." With that phrase, Jesus communicated, "Do not be afraid, you did a good thing."

Jesus told her that the courageous act of merely touching his robe healed her. By saying these words, Jesus praised her for her faith, her bravery, her courage, and her strength to not listen to the rejection of the world. She was able to leave her encounter with Jesus with the reflected appraisal of worthiness to be called Jesus's daughter and friend. We can only imagine how her life changed physically, socially, and spiritually, as she now saw herself as a person of worth and value, as a daughter of the King. From a faith lens, you too can see evidence of God's grace and love when you choose the right reflection to pay attention to.

Unwrapping the Gift of Positive Reflected Appraisal

As children, we are deceived by the rhyme, "Sticks and stones may break my bones, but words will never hurt me." What a lie. Words can cut deeper and do more damage to the soul than any stick or stone ever could. Who has not felt the nauseating punch to the stomach from mean and hurtful words? As a professor, I am not immune to harsh criticism. Whenever I read my student course evaluations at the end of every semester, I fight to not let the negative comments repeat over and over in my head. One semester, I had a class with 24 students. I had 22 very positive reviews and comments. Students noted, "This class changed my life," "Kevin was a blessing to me this semester," and "Wow, just Wow!" I also had two very negative reviews and comments. One student noted that my class was "a waste of their time" and another student wondered, "Why did this school even hire Kevin to teach anyway?" You can guess which reviews I played over and over in my head (and no, it was not the 22 positive comments).

I allowed the two negative reviews to give me the reflected appraisal of my value as a teacher. I felt like an absolute failure. I sought out my mentor and shared my hurt and pain and how I was now convinced I had chosen the wrong profession. My mentor quickly pointed out the 22 students who indicated that I had made the right career choice. I had to choose which reflected appraisal I was going to engage—the negative ones or the positive ones affirming my calling to teach. The negative comments were worth reviewing and learning from (which I did), but they did not need to define me as a teacher or as a person.

My mentor's advice worked, and I not only learned from the negative comments but used them to become a better teacher. It is easy to let the negative messages silence the positive messages. If only we all could hear the words that Jesus spoke to the woman. Despite our flaws and mistakes, Jesus not only calls us sons and daughters, but he also calls us "friends" (see John 15:15).

It can be difficult to hear the positive reflected appraisal of Jesus when the enemy is whispering very convincing negative reflected appraisals in our ears all the time. "How could Jesus love you with all you have done? How could you think you are worthy of being a daughter or son of the King? Why would Jesus die for such a flawed human being as you?" Even though you know the answer to all those negative reflected appraisals, it is easy to forget that Jesus does love you and he did die for you. It is easy to be tempted to look at your reflection in a distorted mirror and see yourself negatively. If you continue to do that, you are unable to see your reflection in the mirror of Jesus's positive appraisal that you are loved unconditionally just the way you are.

It is easy to let the negative appraisals overwhelm you and hurt you to the point that you want to hurt someone else. You then find someone to lash out at with the same negativity that you received. Doing this can make you feel better about yourself briefly, but that feeling will quickly pass since you did not address the real source of your hurt. I used to struggle with this ugly cycle. I listened to so much negativity that it was very hard for me to say kind or positive things to other people. I worked to break this cycle by making myself say one positive thing to a person when I talked to them. After a while, it became easier to say nice and kind statements, and I was able to increase my goal to two positive comments, and then three. Before long, it became much easier to be positive and show a loving appraisal to other people.

The story of the woman's encounter with Jesus is also a reminder of the effect that you can have on other people. Every time you open your mouth and utter a word, or extend a nonverbal look or touch, you communicate to the other person how you see them. You can create a reflected appraisal for every person you encounter. You can use your gift of communication to lift someone up or tear someone down. Your gift of communication comes with this responsibility. As a parent, I have struggled with this responsibility many times. I often find myself wanting to speak to my children in anger for something they have done (and my anger is often quite justified) but I am confronted with having to be accountable for what type of appraisal I communicate. Sometimes, I succeed with my word choice, and sometimes I fail. However, my failures do not define me as a parent, just like my poor course evaluations do not define me as a teacher.

What kind of reflection are you creating with your words? What messages are you sending with a simple glance or touch? Does the other person see God loving them through you, or do you create a reflection that does anything but draw them closer to God?

5 Ways to Unwrap Reflected Appraisal

1. Try to go an entire day without saying anything negative. Be aware that when you speak, you might be reflecting an appraisal of someone to other people. Let your words always be with grace. (Colossians 4:6)

2. In John 15:15, Jesus calls us "friends." Write down the three to five most important qualities of what it means to you to be someone's friend. Look at your list. Is that how you think Jesus sees you? According to his word, it is. Pray and ask God to show you how Jesus is the kind of friend to you that you value.

3. What are the three biggest influences in how you see yourself? (Social media, family, etc.). Is there a balance in how you let these influencers shape your view of yourself? If there is not a balance (one area influences you negatively more than it should), what are some ways you can change that influence?

4. When you take pictures to post on social media platforms, do not pose like a model (Hand on hip, body turned out, etc.). Just smile and click. Do not try to convey an image of a person that you may not be.

5. Write down three to five reasons why you like and use social media. Are those reasons creating a positive or negative reflected appraisal of yourself? Be honest. If you believe some of them are negative, what is a way you can change your use of social media to remove that negative reflected appraisal from your life?

Conclusion

It can be a very sobering thought to realize that every time you open your mouth, you create a reflection that could have extremely long-lasting effects on another person. God has blessed you with his gift of communication. You can use your gift to reflect the Kingdom, or you can misuse your gift to reflect the opposite of the unconditional love of God.

Mirrors can be a helpful part of daily routines and we depend on them in many ways. However, when the mirrors are other peoples' un-Christlike appraisals of you, it is easy to get a distorted picture of yourself, just like a carnival House of Mirrors. Mirrors can give you distorted images of yourself and can quickly remind you of your flaws, blemishes, and imperfections. If it were not for mirrors, you might never think your nose was too big, your eyebrows too thick, your cheekbones not high enough, or your muscles not big enough. Without mirrors, you might never think that you were anything but perfect, just the way God created you.

Just like mirrors are necessary but can reflect negative images, sometimes I see communication in the same way. Communication is necessary for our very survival and can let us display God's love with every word we say. Communication can also be one of the most hurtful, devastating tools we possess. But even when communication is used for negative, evil things, you need to remember that communication remains a gift from God. God intended his gift to be used for good and it can very easily be an incredible blessing in your life. If you can get beyond the hurtful reflections you have received from other people, you might see yourself for the person you are—a daughter or son of the King.

• Prayer Prompt •

Father, thank you again for your gift of communication. Forgive me for the times I have used mirrors to create my identity that have not reflected you or your Kingdom. I pray for the courage and strength to step away from the mirrors that hurt and mislead me and look to you for my true reflected image. Help me to use my gift of communication to communicate you to others through the words I speak and the messages I send. Thank you for calling me "friend." Help me to embrace what that means and to truly understand what it means to be your friend. In Jesus's name, Amen.

Chapter 3: Follow-up Questions

1. What mirrors do you use to "see" yourself?

2. Is there anything from your life (past or present) that was said or done to you that created or creates a negative reflected appraisal of yourself? Who said it and why did their opinion of you matter so much? What are some ways you can surrender that hurt to God?

3. Have you ever thought of or viewed yourself as Jesus's "friend?" Scripture gives us that promise. Is that promise hard to wrap your mind around? Are there any specific ways that you can embrace that promise?

4. Who are some people that you believe put a great deal of value in what you think of them? How do you reflect your appraisal of them with your words? Do you speak with the kindness and love that Jesus showed the sick woman?

5. What are three specific things you can do to create a more positive reflected appraisal for the people you speak to? How can you help them to walk away feeling positive about themselves after a conversation with you?

Chapter 4

Buyer's Regret

Cognitive Dissonance Theory and Luke 10:30–37

People only see what they are prepared to see.[1]

—Ralph Waldo Emerson

FOR MANY YEARS WHILE I WAS GROWING UP, my dad would often comment on other men's gold pocket watches or point out a gold pocket watch he would see in a store that he would love to own. Growing up with meager means, he always wanted a pocket watch but could never justify the expense. When I was age 15, I got my first job bussing tables at a local pie shop. It took me a while, but I eventually saved up enough money for a down payment on a motorcycle I really wanted. Just about the time I had enough money for my dream form of transportation, my dad's 50th birthday came around. While walking through the mall one day looking for a gift for my dad, I saw one of the gold pocket watches in a store window that he had been eyeing. Of course, the price of the watch was the exact same amount I had saved for my motorcycle. I got a knot in my stomach and I felt conflicted. I pondered, "Should I get my dad the pocket watch he always wanted or buy myself a motorcycle?" I asked a few friends and the advice, by consensus, was to buy my dad the pocket watch, telling me I would feel much better if I did. After thinking it over, I returned to the mall and bought my dad the gold pocket watch. The feeling I had as I watched him open the gift and cry made me feel guilty that I had ever considered not buying the watch in the first place.

It is not uncommon in our everyday activities to find ourselves having to make decisions that create internal conflicts. Sometimes, as people of faith, we see a need someone has, and we feel conflicted as we contemplate whether to meet the need. This internal struggle we feel is called cognitive dissonance—the presence of two conflicting pieces of information that forces us to make a choice. This chapter will define cognitive dissonance, explore an example of cognitive dissonance from Scripture, and finally, examine some steps to take to navigate cognitive dissonance in our relationships.

Cognitive Dissonance

According to psychologist and researcher Leon Festinger, cognitive dissonance is, "The distressing mental state that people feel when they find themselves doing things that do not fit with what they know or having opinions that do not fit with other opinions they hold."[2] This means that when you receive information that contradicts a belief or value you have, it creates a form of mental stress or discomfort that is hard for you to live with. Your mind needs to resolve this tension, because "the tension of dissonance motivates us to change either our behavior or our belief in an effort to avoid that distressing feeling."[3] It is like looking at an incredible dessert in a high-end restaurant. In your mind, you know you should not eat the dessert because it is filled with fat and calories, but the visual presentation of the dessert provides you conflicting information. You think, "How could something so beautiful be so bad for you?"

Not all cognitive dissonance is as simple as whether or not to eat a dessert. Sometimes, you are confronted by conflicting information or competing expectations in your daily relationships, and you struggle with communicating the tension created by that conflict. Sometimes the tension is created by something someone does. If I were to walk up to you and say "Hi" and stick out my hand to you, I would expect you to respond by saying "Hi" and reaching out and shaking my hand. If you did not respond the way I expected and just stood there and stared at me, that would create tension between us. I would have conflicting pieces of information. In my mind, I think, "I was always taught in our culture to say *Hi* and shake the other person's hand. This person is not shaking my hand and saying *Hi*." These thoughts in my mind create tension, and since I generally do not enjoy feeling tension, I try to figure out the reason for the behavior so I can make sense of it. I could give the person the benefit of the doubt and think, "They must not know about the cultural expectation of saying *Hi* and shaking hands. OK, I can forgive them." This act of forgiveness relieves the tension, and I can now engage in my relationship with the other person. Or I could choose to think, "What a jerk, why did they not shake my hand, what is wrong with them, they are a horrible person." I resolve the tension I feel by attacking and blaming them for the miscommunication. If I choose this option, there is a good chance the relationship will suffer.

The tension in the relationship can also be created by political, social, or religious values and beliefs. I can meet a person and find out that they are a person of faith and attend a local church. Because I perceive that the two of us share a faith-based belief system, I expect us to have similar theological opinions and ideas. But when we start talking to each other, the other person expresses a theological belief that differs from my theological belief and it creates tension, or cognitive dissonance, in our relationship. I thought the other person believed "A" only to find out they believe "B." I now feel uncomfortable and need to resolve the perceived tension. I could choose to navigate the tension in several ways. I could dismiss the person as not being serious about their faith and decide we cannot be friends. I could ask them what they meant by the statement and explore ways to better understand them. Or I could choose to ignore the difference and accept our disagreement. Whatever scenario I choose, I ameliorate the tension (the cognitive dissonance) that the disagreement created.

Cognitive dissonance is bound to arrive in just about every relationship because not every person thinks or believes the exact same things. As a result, no matter how much you feel you are like another person, you are eventually going to disagree about something. The greater the importance of the issue to you and the greater the discrepancy, the greater the magnitude of the dissonance you will feel.[4] If you have a strong conviction about a theological topic, such as baptism, based upon your upbringing and training, but one day a friend who is a person of faith expresses a conviction that contradicts that belief, you will experience cognitive dissonance. You would have two competing pieces of information that did not match. If you believed your view on baptism to be foundational to your faith, then you would experience especially strong cognitive dissonance. You would have to choose from several options to resolve the tension. You could defend your original position and refuse to accept the new perspective, or you could change your position on baptism to the new perspective and abandon your original view. You could also choose to find a way to join the two perspectives together. There might also be other options to resolve the mental tension you are feeling. Since you want to maintain a positive relationship with the person you are talking to, you need to address any tension you feel building inside of you. If the tension is not addressed, the tension can cause you to react in a negative manner, hurting your relationship with the other person. You have a choice to try to resolve the tension and save the relationship or ignore the tension possibly at the expense of the relationship.

One way to reduce the tension is to refuse to accept the new information. This is a common response because "people avoid information that is likely to increase dissonance."[5] This is the "stick your fingers in your ears and sing la-la-la-la-la" approach. This approach usually involves only listening to opinions and selecting reading material that is consistent with your existing beliefs, and the tendency to choose to only be around people who think the same way. Researchers call this behavior confirmation bias, when humans discount information that contradicts past judgments.[6] The danger in doing so is that you may end up believing and acting on falsehoods because you refuse to test your original assumptions against new information. It is difficult to be stretched and grow outside your comfort zone when you avoid information that contradicts your own beliefs. This mindset can drive you away from people who think differently than you do. I once heard a speaker claim, "If you are not listening to the people who make you uncomfortable, then you are not listening to the right people." It is very hard to be willing to risk our own beliefs to listen and engage with people who see the world differently than you do.

Not all cognitive dissonance is derived from theological issues. Many issues of everyday life, from the food you eat (like selecting a dessert), to the clothes you wear (how can it be inappropriate when it is so stylish?), to the car you buy (I want that powerful engine, but it gets horrible gas mileage), can all create cognitive dissonance. You feel stress and tension when making a decision and are often torn about what you do decide. In your relationships, cognitive dissonance can take many forms, such as when good friends say critical or mean things about other people and you feel that is wrong. Do you say something and risk their rejection, or do you stay quiet? If you are dating someone and discover they have opposite political views from you, do you continue dating and just ignore the dissonance or do you decide that the relationship cannot survive this opposition and break it off? The greater the dissonance, the greater the chance to regret your decision. You talk yourself into ordering the dessert, only to feel guilty and promise to spend an extra 20 minutes at the gym the next day. You continue dating the person and are on edge all the time hoping that political topics never arise in your conversations. Feeling on edge all the time around that person now makes you regret not addressing the problem sooner. Through the lens of cognitive dissonance theory, you can see how internal contradictions directly affect how you live and communicate in your daily life.

Luke 10:30–37 and The Good Samaritan

As people of faith, we encounter cognitive dissonance every day as we struggle to live a life that honors God. The struggle to make decisions that honor your relationship with God is real and can create cognitive dissonance in ways you never imagined. Jesus provided an excellent lens for people of faith to use to resolve cognitive dissonance and honor God in the story of the Good Samaritan recorded in Luke 10:30–37. As Luke recounts:

> In reply Jesus said: "A man was going down from Jerusalem to Jericho, when he was attacked by robbers. They stripped him of his clothes, beat him and went away, leaving him half dead. A priest happened to be going down the same road, and when he saw the man, he passed by on the other side. So too, a Levite, when he came to the place and saw him, passed by on the other side. But a Samaritan, as he traveled, came where the man was; and when he saw him, he took pity on him. He went to him and bandaged his wounds, pouring on oil and wine. Then he put the man on his own donkey, brought him to an inn and took care of him. The next day he took out two denarii and gave them to the innkeeper. 'Look after him,' he said, 'and when I return, I will reimburse you for any extra expense you may have.' "Which of these three do you think was a neighbor to the man who fell into the hands of robbers?" The expert in the law replied, "The one who had mercy on him." Jesus told him "Go and do likewise."

Jesus described three different men, all of whom experienced conflicting mental messages or cognitive dissonance. The first man to pass by the beaten man was a priest who passed on the other side. We are not told why he passed on the other side; he just did. Something caused the priest to move away from the injured man. The priest may have experienced some sort of dissonance. He may have been afraid, in a hurry, or not want to get involved in the situation. He may have thought that touching the man would make him ritually unclean, conflicting with his role in temple service. Whatever the reason, instead of focusing on the big picture—the image of God in a fellow human being in need—he focused on narrow factors that created an internal contradiction. Crossing to the other side addressed his dissonance, even if only temporarily.

The second man to pass by was a Levite, a trained Hebrew religious leader. Again, the story does not include an explanation as to why he passed to the other side. He just did. Something about the situation created cognitive dissonance for him, and he chose to resolve the tension by passing to the other side of the road instead of finding resolution in the love and mercy of God.

The third person to pass by was a Samaritan. The detail that many biblical scholars point out in this story is that the Samaritan is a person from whom the Jewish man had no right to expect any help or relief because of the enmity which existed between the two nations.[7] The Samaritan had to have felt a sense of, "This person is an outsider, so I am not going to get involved, I am just going to mind my own business." He likely had cognitive dissonance between the enmity of ethnic division and the call of compassion to help a hurting human being. He chose to resolve the tension by focusing on the man's humanity. Not only did he help, but he also took care of the man, paid for his lodging, and promised to cover any other additional expenses. He knew the right thing to do, and he did it. No regrets, no wavering, he was called to help, and he acted. Compassion for another human being enabled him to overcome the dissonance of Jew versus Samaritan. We can only imagine how this act by the Samaritan impacted not only the Jewish man's life, but also the life of the Samaritan. Through the lens of this beautiful parable, you can see how people of faith can resolve dissonance and communicate with "outsiders."

Unwrapping the Gift of Communication in Response to Cognitive Dissonance

It is easy to miss opportunities for service or God-ordained relationships because of cognitive dissonance. When you come upon a person asking for money, it is not uncommon to immediately feel tension. As a person of faith, your teaching, your training, or your calling to love others tells you to stop, help, and give. However, there is often that little nagging voice that screams "Walk the other way, cross to the other side, stay away!" You quickly try to resolve the tension by thinking "Oh, they can get help from someone else," or "They might try to rob me," or "They might be carrying a disease" to justify not stopping. When you meet a socially awkward person, you think, "Be nice," and say, "Hi, how are you?" hoping and praying they do not take you seriously and tell you how they are. Your true motivation is to appear as if you care, but your primary thought is, "How fast can I get away from this person?" When someone strikes up a friendly conversation with you, it is easy to think, "What do they want to sell me?" and try to get away. These thoughts and behaviors only cause you to "wrap up" your gift of communication rather than "unwrap" it as this book has tried to teach.

I was once visiting a large megachurch that held several services on Sunday mornings. The pastor announced from the pulpit that they were going to have to discontinue childcare during some of the services because there just was not enough help. The congregants had become so complacent in their attendance that many of them expected someone else to serve because they had too much to do. People of faith are called to serve, yet, when the call interferes with selfish ways, it is easy to rationalize the problem away to relieve the tension.

You also experience cognitive dissonance in your personal relationships daily. Disagreements with co-workers, friends, significant others, or spouses are going to happen as you interact, talk, and share about your life. As a person of faith, how you choose to use your gift of communication to resolve your dissonance is very important. God holds you accountable for the words you use when you speak to other people.[8] When someone in your life expresses a belief, idea, or value that differs from yours, it is easy to feel threatened by the dissonance that disagreement can cause. One of the easiest approaches to resolving tension is to attack the other person. They were wrong, you were right, and you will fight to defend your position. It is not wrong to have a firm belief system, but if you are so sure you are right, then why does someone disagreeing with you make you so defensive? You may also choose to resolve the tension by judging the other person's beliefs and being very critical of them. Unfortunately, many people of faith choose this option on certain theological beliefs, and not only are relationships severed, but churches are divided, and hate takes over. I have been a part of more than one congregation that split over a particular issue. It was very sad to see and experience, and I always struggle to see where God was honored when it happened.

Of course, there are other approaches. You can ask the other person questions to have them share their ideas and gain more information (part of good communication covered in Chapter 2). Even if you still disagree, you can convey love to them as Christ commanded (see John 15:12). You can identify the tension you are feeling as a natural part of communication and cognitive dissonance and not fear the tension because God loves both of you. It is never easy to live with tension in relationships, but when you better understand the reason for that tension, it becomes more manageable. You can choose to use confirming language over disconfirming language, which is explained in greater detail in Chapter 10. When I speak to another person, I have choices over the words I use. There is a difference between saying "You are wrong" and "I have come to feel differently about that topic but that does not prevent us from talking."

Some topics may be non-negotiable to you for a certain type of relationship. I have a close neighbor who has a very different theological belief system than I do, but that does not keep us from being good neighbors. However, when I met my wife, discovering her faith journey and making sure we were both on the same page regarding certain theological issues was extremely important to me. I wanted a marriage where our faith journeys were similar. If my wife had the same theological beliefs as my neighbor, I would not have married her. There would have been too much tension from our disagreements. My closer friends have similar beliefs and values to mine, but I also have friends who differ from me a great deal. Because I see them through the eyes of Christ as fellow human beings whom God loves, the cognitive dissonance (and subsequent tension) is tolerable, manageable, and understood as being a normal part of communication.

5 Ways to Unwrap Your Gift of Communication in Response to Cognitive Dissonance

1. Understand that cognitive dissonance is a normal part of any relationship. Because you are uniquely you, you will never agree with another person 100%. Accept that there will be differences.

2. Realize that you have choices in how you express the tension you feel. You can judge and criticize, or you can love and be kind.

3. Accept that you may have non-negotiable values and beliefs that you may not share with another person. Those beliefs do not have to limit all your relationships (friends or neighbors) but it is OK if they limit some (spouse).

4. If you are experiencing tension from a decision you made, chances are you may not have followed your calling as a person of faith. Resist the

temptation to turn your back on whatever you are feeling, and do the right thing. Remember, the right thing is often the hardest thing to do, but it will always be the right thing.

5. If you have managed cognitive dissonance tension poorly in the past, that is fine. Forgive yourself, ask God to forgive you, then commit to handling it differently and better in the future. Make a note to specifically use tools from this book to communicate in your relationships in a way that honors God.

Conclusion

Experiencing tension in a relationship is a normal and natural part of the communication process. Understanding how and why you have this tension is a good first step to better navigating the tension in your relationships. You are responsible for how you use your gift of communication, and the words you use to communicate your tension with another person are very important. Fortunately, you have choices. This book is designed to help you by putting more tools in your toolbox, so you have more options and ideas for God-honoring ways to use your gift of communication.

I often wrestle with this tension in my own relationships. Sometimes I find it hard to put other people before my own feelings. I remember one day I was passing through the Student Union after a long meeting. I was anxious to get off campus for some peace and quiet when I heard a voice from across the room call out my name, "Kevin." I glanced in the direction of the voice, waved, pointed at my watch to indicate I was pressed for time, and jetted out the door. A few days later, I found out the student had been looking for someone to talk to. Earlier that day, their parents had cut them off and disowned them because of their faith. They had no money and no place to live. They needed someone to talk to, but I was too self-absorbed to be that person. I have never in my life felt as low or guilty as I did when I found out why she called out my name. It took me a long time to forgive myself (and I am not sure if I have fully forgiven myself). Her voice calling my name created cognitive dissonance for me and I resolved the dissonance with a quick wave and exiting the building. All I accomplished with my choices was to create even greater dissonance when I discovered the reason why. Rather than chose to be the Samaritan, I chose to be the priest and the Levite.

We are not told what the priest or Levite felt or experienced after they crossed to the other side. We can only wonder what type of regret they may have felt. We can easily imagine the feeling the Samaritan had, probably something like what I experienced when I watched my dad open his gift to find his new gold pocket watch. And to be honest, my dad never would have let me buy a motorcycle anyway.

• Prayer Prompt •

Father, thank you for our gift of communication, even though it can be hard to use your gift wisely. Forgive me for when I have felt tension in a relationship and attacked or criticized the other person. I pray for wisdom and insight on how to experience tension in relationships but not damage the relationship with the way I communicate the tension. Help me love the people around me with my words no matter what we agree or disagree on. Thank you for hearing my prayers. In Jesus's name, Amen.

Chapter Four: Follow-Up Questions

1. Have you ever experienced cognitive dissonance when trying to buy something like a new car, furniture, or something else? What was the tension you felt and how did you resolve it?

2. Have you ever experienced cognitive dissonance with your faith? Have you struggled to do the right thing when you see a need such as a person asking for money or a need in your church? Did you experience any "buyer's regret" as a result?

3. How easy is it for you to be in a relationship with someone who has different beliefs or values than you have? Have you experienced a severed relationship because the tension from the dissonance was so great the relationship could not survive? What happened?

4. How can you offer your time or resources to help someone like the beaten man in Luke 10:30–37? Is there a relationship in your life that could use some attention, even if it means having to resolve some cognitive dissonance?

5. Have you ever experienced cognitive dissonance with someone or something and acted negatively in response? What was it, how did you mishandle it, and how might you change your approach now?

Chapter 5

It Is OK Not to Be OK

Communicating Emotions and the Psalms

Unexpressed emotions will never die. They are buried alive and will come forth later in uglier ways.[1]

—Sigmund Freud

We try so hard to hide everything we're really feeling from those who probably need to know our true feelings the most. People try to bottle up their emotions, as if it's somehow wrong to have natural reactions to life.[2]

—Colleen Hoover

MANY YEARS AGO, WHEN MY SON was five years old, I took him with me to the grocery store. He was sitting in the child's seat in the grocery cart facing me as I pushed the cart. When I entered the checkout lane at the completion of my shopping trip, I did not see that my son had moved his hands from the bar right in front of him and facing me, to the sides of the cart. As I was unloading the groceries onto the conveyor belt, the shopping cart got pushed up against the side of the checkout counter and my son's fingers on the hand that was holding the side of the cart got smashed between the cart and the counter. I heard him scream and start crying and I looked to see what had happened. I instantly felt horrible for pushing the cart up against the counter and quickly picked him up to hold and comfort him. I held him, apologized profusely, and encouraged him to cry and let out his hurt.

The person standing in line in front of me and the cashier (both of whom were women) immediately began to give me tips on how to get him to stop crying. I thought it was odd to expect a 5-year-old to not cry after getting their fingers smashed, so I thanked them both but continued to hold my son and let him cry. His little fingers got smashed by the counter and it hurt.

If that happened to me, I would scream and cry too. I did not understand why the two women were so focused on getting my son to stop crying.

As I reflected on the incident later that day, I saw the two women's approach to my son's emotions to be how many people approach the expression of emotions, especially by males, to discourage or even try to stop the expression of the emotion. This approach seems especially true if the emotion is seen as negative or bad. Realistically, God did not create us with only positive emotions like happiness and joy; we were given emotions like anger and frustration as well. Yet, most of the admonition we receive is to only express our positive emotions. I have heard many sermons and read many teachings on how people of faith are to experience and express joy and happiness, but I do not recall ever hearing any sermons or reading anything about how people of faith are supposed to express negative emotions like depression, anxiety, or fear.

Since you are created in the image of God and that means you are given a gift of communication along with a full range of emotions, a conversation about how people of faith communicate their emotions is warranted. This chapter will explore some of the theories about how we communicate our emotions, examine a little of what the Bible offers regarding emotions, and provide some ways you can communicate emotions in a healthy way.

Understanding Emotions

Emotions can be incredibly complicated and misunderstood. Perhaps one of the biggest misunderstandings is thinking that there are "male" emotions and "female" emotions, when in fact psychological research does not support this idea.[3] According to Scripture God created us all, male and female, in his image which includes the full spectrum of emotions. Somewhere along the line, it seems like there became rules on which gender can acceptably communicate which emotions. I have often wondered if my son had been a girl when he smashed his fingers at the grocery store, would the people around us have been so quick to offer ways to get him to stop? When I was a young boy myself, I got beaten up by a boy down the street. I ran home and told my father, and I was immediately told, "Be a man and stop crying." Then my father took me into the backyard to teach me how to fight. There was something about my gender that made it wrong to feel and express certain emotions with tears, but OK to express those feelings with my fists.

This sentiment is not exclusive to how I was raised by my father. Years ago, I attended a men's retreat with my church and in the very first session, the speaker (promoted as a "man's man"—whatever that means) told a story of how he had been talking to another man when the other man started to cry. The speaker declared that the crying man, "Had the emotions of a girl." Not only was the comment unfairly critical of women, but the speaker made it sound like there was something wrong with a man who was crying. I wanted to raise my hand and ask the speaker if he had ever read John 11:35, "Jesus wept"!?[4] Jesus did not just cry, he wept. If Jesus felt emotions and wept, why is the communication of a sad emotion through crying something that is bad or wrong just because I am male?

If I am taught as a child to express certain emotions in certain ways, then it becomes the communication pattern that I resort to as an adult. If crying is bad and not "What a man does," then when I am a man and I feel an emotion that evokes crying, I will need to find another way to express that emotion. Quite often the alternative method of expression may involve acting out physically (like fighting the way my father taught me). When I look at the statistics of the amount of domestic violence in the United States, I cannot help but believe that some of this ugly scar upon our culture is created by our own doing. If a boy is taught to "be tough, be a man, don't cry" when he feels hurt and pain, what does he do when he is an adult and feels those very same emotions of hurt and pain? He only knows to stop crying and fight.

Perhaps some of the confusion about the communication of emotions comes from how easy it can be to mismanage them. Emotions are very powerful, and I am sure you have experienced a time when another person expressed their emotions around you so strongly that you ended up absorbing their emotion. I have often been in a good mood, and when someone comes into my office and starts complaining and grumbling about a certain topic with such negativity that by the time they leave I am no longer in a good mood. I am grumbling and negative and the topic did not even affect me. The process by which emotions are transferred like this from one person to another as though they were some kind of social virus is referred to by psychologists and communication scholars as emotional contagion.[5] his transfer process is applicable to all emotions, not just negative ones. We are seldom bothered when a person is so positive, happy, joyful, or peaceful that they transfer those positive emotions to us. Who does not want to be lifted up or feel happier? But what about when the act of communication (spewing negativity) leaves us feeling yucky and down, who wants to be around that person?

Emotions, Jesus, God, and the Psalms

God created everyone as emotional beings. You are made in the likeness of God, and God is an emotional being. God feels human emotions like anger[6] and joy.[7] In the New Testament, Jesus experienced emotions as a human. God, Jesus, human beings—all three are emotional beings. In the gospels, Jesus is credited with exhibiting emotions such as despair,[8] anger,[9] sorrow,[10] frustration,[11] patience,[12] fear,[13] rebuke,[14] sadness,[15] impatience,[16] displeasure,[17] grief,[18] compassion,[19] and agony.[20] The Book of Psalms provides wonderful examples of how both God and the Psalmists experienced and felt emotions. God is identified as experiencing the emotions of mercy,[21] kindness,[22] anger,[23] gentleness,[24] love,[25] pleasure,[26] and compassion.[27] When writing the psalms, the authors identified a wide range of emotions they experienced and either used the emotion as motivation to write the psalm or expressed the emotion in the psalm. Some of the emotions the human authors identified were anxiety,[28] sorrow,[29] hope,[30] joy,[31] despair,[32] fear,[33] anger,[34] remorse,[35] desire,[36] trust,[37] shame,[38] mourning,[39] delight,[40] distress,[41] and happiness.[42] Emotions are a crucial piece of being human and learning how to use your gift of communication to convey emotions in a healthy way is very important, but can also be very challenging.

I would propose that some of the confusion around navigating emotions lies in the myth that all people of faith are to live in a constant state of joy and happiness. That does not seem realistic to me, nor does it fit the picture we see in Scripture. Emotions are a natural reaction to life: feeling joy, happiness, anger, and anxiety are all part of being human. But when negative emotions are expressed so strongly and become an emotional contagion, that perpetuates the negative stigma around so-called bad emotions. If a person walks into a room and they are bubbling with positive feelings and those feelings rub off on you, very few people are going to complain about this behavior. However, if a person walks into a room in a foul mood and within minutes you are feeling in a foul mood as well, that is not a positive experience.

Negative emotions can be incredibly powerful and difficult to manage if you are not taught at a young age to express them in a constructive way. While Scripture does not direct you to never feel or express a negative emotion, you are given some parameters on how you are supposed to express those emotions. Chapter 12 will explore in greater depth how to communicate anger. The key to expressing anger, or any negative emotion, lies in how you express that emotion. When your expression of an emotion crosses a certain line, it can become sin. Note, I did not write that any negative emotion is a sin. Far from it. The Book of Psalms identifies many emotions in God that could be considered negative. The same argument can be made for some of the emotions Jesus showed in the New Testament. From a faith perspective, you can see that the emotions you experience are not bad; it is how you choose to express those emotions that causes trouble.

Unwrapping Communicating Emotions

Determining where to draw the line between healthy and unhealthy emotional expression is not a simple endeavor. However, there are some filters I would propose to help you navigate your emotions. First, sometimes it is difficult to distinguish between what it was that triggered your emotion versus the person who engaged the trigger. If a person says or does something that upsets you, it is natural to blame the person and attack them. It is easy to lash out and exclaim, "You make me so angry!" when the truth is, it was the person's statement that made you angry. This is especially true when it is a person who is close to you. I love my wife and the many qualities that make her who she is. However, now and then, she can say something that is hurtful to me. It is what she said, at that moment, that caused me to feel upset, not the totality of who she is. I fell in love with her and asked her to marry me because of who she is as a person. When she does say something that bothers me, it does not change any of the reasons why I fell in love with her. All those characteristics are still there. So, blurting, "You make me so mad!" misrepresents the situation. I need to specify, "I was not comfortable when you said my tie was ugly." The key is to focus on the object of your emotion, not the person.

This act is commonly referred to by psychologists and communication researchers as using "I" language. "I" language shows that the speaker takes responsibility for the concern or critique by describing his or her reaction to the other's behavior without making any judgments about its worth. Using "I" language allows the speaker to clearly express their thoughts, feelings, and wants.[43] In the example above regarding if my wife says something that bothers me, using "I" language means I do not blame her for my emotion.

If I feel angry, I say, "I am angry," I identify the source of my anger, "I did not appreciate it when you called me that name," and I do not blame her for "making" me angry. If I choose to be hurt and angered by her words, then that is on me. The problem with not using "I" language is that as soon as I attack my wife because I blame her for my anger (for example, "You shut up!"), my response guarantees a defensive response from her, and the conversation has nowhere to go but down. I need to take ownership of my emotions—why? Because they are *my* emotions. When both people in the conversation take ownership of their emotions, both parties are on offense and not defense, trying to blame the other person for the emotions they are feeling. Can my wife say something that arouses an emotion? Yes, of course. But it is still my emotional state that I am experiencing. I am responsible for my emotions. If I cannot identify, name, and express that emotion, then I need to get some help to learn how to do so.

A second step you can use to foster healthy emotional expression is to understand what it means to take ownership of your own emotions. Just as the first step above admonished you to identify the object of your emotion, it is equally important to remember that you are responsible for your own emotions. It is not the job of other people to make you feel happy or feel good about yourself. You are responsible for your own happiness and feeling good about yourself. It is not my wife's job to make me feel good about myself. I am responsible for feeling good about myself. That does not mean that it is OK for her to ignore me or say horrible things to me. Of course not. What it means is that I did not marry her because I expected her to make me feel good about myself. I married her because she had the character qualities I was looking for in someone to be my partner through life.

I get nervous whenever someone tells me they got engaged, and I ask them, "Why do you want to marry that person?" and they respond, "I like the way he makes me feel," or "I like the way I feel when I am with her." This is scary to me because I wonder what happens one day when they wake up and they do not feel good about themselves, and being with that person no longer makes them feel good about themselves. It becomes easy to blame the other person for their unhappiness. They may think, "You used to make me feel good about myself. You no longer do that. What happened? You've changed, I am not sure I know who you are anymore. I want a divorce."

If I enter a relationship knowing that I am responsible for my own emotions, then when I struggle emotionally, I know I am responsible for attending to my emotional needs rather than placing that responsibility on another person. This process is known as the rational-emotive approach to managing emotions.[44] According to this approach, the key to expressing emotions in a positive way is to remove the unproductive mental processes we easily fall prey to. When I enter relationships expecting other people to be responsible for my emotional state, I am in an unproductive mindset. If I am dependent upon other people to make me happy, then I will never be a happy person. Other people are not capable of always making me happy. It will always be a temporary state. Years ago, I found myself looking for a person who would always make me happy. Once I realized that was an effort in futility, I sought professional help and learned how to use my faith as my foundation for happiness. I no longer depend upon other people for my emotional state.

This mindset allows me to express my emotions in a positive way. I do not expect my wife to make me happy, so when she says something that hurts my feelings, I can separate the object of my emotion (what she said) from the person who said it (my wife). I can tell her, "When you said X, Y, Z, I felt hurt," not "You make me so mad!" which is sure to generate a defensive response from her since I am attacking her as a person.

We express healthy emotions when we understand the difference between feeling emotions and acting on those emotions. Just because you feel an emotion does not mean you have to express the emotion. This is perhaps the hardest of all the ways we can express emotions in a healthy way. When we feel wronged, hurt, or attacked, our emotions run high. Our heartbeat races or we may get butterflies in our stomachs—we react physiologically to the event. Emotional maturity manifests itself in a person's ability to hold their tongue or walk away from a situation that is escalating. There have been times when my children have said or done something, and I have become very upset with them. I feel very angry, but if I act and speak at that moment, I know I will cross the line and sin. I have to say, "I am too angry right now to talk about this. I need to walk away, and we will talk about this in an hour." Remember, Ephesians 4:26 does not instruct us to never be angry; but rather indicates that while it is OK to feel the emotion of anger, we are not to sin in how we express that anger (see Chapter 12 for more on navigating anger).

Finally, one of the best tools we can remember to use when navigating emotions is to never tell another person how to feel. I am always amused when I hear someone tell another person, "Don't be angry" When was the last time you were angry or upset and another person said to you, "Don't be upset" and you immediately went from huffing and puffing to, "OK, you're right, I'm OK now" and you stopped huffing and puffing? I am willing to bet that has never happened to you. So, if it does not work on you, then why do you try it on other people? Always try to validate the emotion you hear in the words or the delivery of the person expressing their emotion. Statements like, "You sound really upset," or "I can hear in your voice that you are really frustrated" can go a long way toward de-escalating a situation rather than escalating it. Validating an emotion does not mean you have to agree with the other person. A person can tell you they are very angry with someone, and the cause of that anger may seem petty or minor to you. Rather than diminish the emotions of the other person by saying, "Why are you so mad, that seems silly" (guaranteed to get a defensive response), validate the emotion you hear in their words or voice by saying, "You sound very upset about this." This response will usually help de-escalate a situation as the other person will feel validated and not defensive.

5 Ways to Unwrap Communicating Emotions

1. Never tell another person how to feel. Validate the emotion you hear in their voice and words. Comments such as "You sound very upset" or "You sound very hurt by this," will be received much better than telling someone "Don't be upset."

2. Identify the object of your emotion. A "person" does not upset you; it is usually something that was said or done that caused the emotional reaction. So, name what it was: "When you called me that name, it really hurt my feelings."

3. Focus on "I" language. Avoid telling someone, "You make me so angry!" when it was something the other person said or did that caused you to feel angry. Explain, "I feel angry when you call me that name."

4. Understand the difference between feeling and acting. Just because you feel upset does not always mean you have to act upset. The more mature your emotional understanding, the easier it is to separate the two behaviors.

5. If you were raised either to repress your emotions or to express them by acting out, seek help. Learn how to identify and express your emotions in a healthy way. All emotions are a part of being human and

made in the image of God, but we need to learn how to communicate our emotions in a healthy way.

Conclusion

Emotions, just like communication, can be a confusing gift from God. We are made in the image of God, which means we are blessed with emotions that cover a wide range of feelings and expressions. Each one of us has been raised in different environments, so the communication of our emotions can vary a great deal. I was raised in a home where emotions were not talked about or expressed in healthy ways. As a result, when I became an adult, I had to get counseling and relearn what emotions were all about and how to express them in a healthy way—even the negative ones. I have tried hard to raise my son in an environment where the healthy expression of emotions is encouraged and expected, even if it means letting him cry in the grocery store checkout lane when his fingers get smashed by the cart.

Emotions are powerful and contagious. One person can have the power to change the entire climate in a room, sometimes in a very negative way. This type of emotional contagion is not why God gave you emotions. You need to choose to name your emotions and understand when and how to express your feelings in a positive way.

• Prayer Prompt •

Father, thank you for your gift of communication. Thank you for giving us the ability to feel and have emotions. Your gift of emotions allows us to love, to care, and to feel in our relationships. Your gift also allows us to fall prey to fear, hurt, and pain. These emotions are real, but they can cripple us without our even realizing it. We can project our negative emotions onto others, intentionally or unintentionally, and not honor you by those actions. Forgive me when I have failed to manage my emotions in a way that honors you. Forgive me for the times I have used my emotions to lash out or try to hurt someone for what I perceived as a wrong toward me. That is not why you gave us emotions. I pray for the courage to know how to express and when to act on my emotions and the strength to do what is right. This is not easy, so I turn to you for help, Lord. In Jesus's name, Amen.

Chapter 5: Follow-Up Questions

1. Reflect on how you were taught as a child to express your emotions. Did your gender affect what you were taught? Were you told that certain emotions were bad and should not be expressed?

2. What negative emotions do you find hard to express in a healthy way? What are three things you can do to navigate how to express those emotions in a more positive way?

3. Do you know a person who has a reputation for spreading negative emotional contagion? Why do you think they choose to express their feelings in this way?

4. How easy is it to take full ownership of our own emotions, to engage the rational emotive approach, and not depend on other people for our feelings? Is it a realistic expectation?

5. What are three ways you can help create a positive emotional contagion environment in any of the different groups or organizations you experience daily. Are there any groups or organizations that you feel you just cannot help to become more positive? Why or why not?

Chapter 6

You Just Do Not Understand!

The Languages of Rapport Talk,
Report Talk, and James 3:8

The sum of human wisdom is not contained in any one language,
and no single language is capable of expressing all forms and degrees of human comprehension.[1]

—Ezra Pound

I GREW UP IN SOUTHERN CALIFORNIA learning a language style that reflected the beach culture. Statements like, "Dude, surf's up." or "The waves were
totally gnarly today," were very common among my high school friends.
When I went to graduate school, I attended a university in southern Louisiana and had to learn a whole new language system. Much of my Southern
California language was no longer useful. There were no "Dudes" in Louisiana. I learned the world of French/Creole language with words such as
"lagniappe" which meant, "an extra gift given in a transaction that was not
expected by the terms of the contract."[2] I heard this term applied to everything from classroom exams to Sunday dinner.[3] I now teach at a school in
northern Oregon where there are neither "dudes" nor "lagniappe."

With each culture I have lived in, I had to learn a new language system.
In Chapter 1 of this book, I explained how humans are born with the gift
of the creation of language. However, all language systems must be learned.
A child born in France is not born speaking French: they are born with the
ability to learn and use language, and French is the language they learn because that is the language of their culture. The same is true for a child born
in Germany, Mexico, or many other countries in the world. When we learn
one language system, it can be difficult to realize that not all cultures use the
same language system, even within the boundaries of the same country. I
experienced the culture shock of different language systems when I moved

from Southern California to southern Louisiana. I went through another language culture shock when I moved to northern Oregon.

Every time I learned a new language system, I better understood each new culture. The language I learned helped to shape my view of the world considering how the people in that culture viewed the world. In Southern California, I knew what a "Dude" was. In southern Louisiana, I knew how to ask for something "extra." The language of the culture both reflected and shaped the worldviews of those cultures. Theorists refer to this function of language as "linguistic relativity."[4] Think for a minute about the culture (the area and/or the people) where you live. You can probably identify some of the language that makes your culture unique (like "dudes" or "lagniappe"). What you might not think about is how your language system may also reflect how you were raised, what religious environment you experienced, or even the personality types of the people who surrounded you as a child. Language plays an important role in any culture and our relationships within cultures.

There are numerous ways to study language. Children spend years learning the correct use of grammar and language rules ("Don't dangle that participle!"). Language study also includes understanding phonetics, diction, and articulation. It can also include word meanings or the difference between similar-sounding words (to, too, and two). Language study may also include looking at the pragmatics of daily discourse. But since the goal of this book, and thus this chapter, is healthier relationships, I want to focus on two types of language patterns that many people learn—rapport talk versus report talk. These language patterns are very different and express how a person sees the role of communication in their world. Understanding your preferred language style can help you better understand other people. The goal of this chapter, then, is to explore what type of language style you prefer, what the Bible provides to help guide you through your language choices, and how your language style of choice affects the way you communicate in your relationships.

Report versus Rapport Talk

How you were raised, your religious environment, or the personality types of the people around you while growing up reflect just a few of the many influences on your language development. I know many people raised in a faith-based home where swearing was not allowed. To those individuals, a person who swears is perceived as not very "holy" or "right with God." However, I know other individuals from faith-based homes who see nothing wrong with swearing and do not see it as a barometer of a person's relationship with God. This example demonstrates how the language of the religious culture you were raised in can be different. Imagine all the other areas of your life that language has affected, especially the many different relationships in your life.

Additionally, based on the culture you were raised in, you may see the purpose and use of language to serve a different purpose. Linguist Deborah Tannen studied conversations between people and developed the theory that some people use language as a form of "Report Talk" while other people use language as a form of "Rapport Talk."[5]

Report talkers see the purpose of language and communication as maintaining position, power, and status in a relationship. Report talkers like to provide useful information that facilitates problem-solving when addressing a task. Often, a report talker sees themselves as an individual in a hierarchical social order in which they must display their knowledge to one-up another person. For them, communication is a tool of negotiation people use to try and achieve and maintain the upper hand.[6] At the same time, they may get a great deal of pleasure in being able to provide information that is useful and helpful to other people. When a report talker is asked, "How was your day?" they will use language to give you facts rather than emotional connection. The language might be simple like just responding with, "Fine." This response answers the question but reveals very little about personal challenges or emotions. On the other hand, since information is often viewed as a source of power, a report talker may like to talk about their positive experiences and accomplishments to show their credibility. By focusing primarily on information that reflects well on their knowledge and competence, a report talker is able to avoid talking about weaknesses and/or feelings, which can be perceived as not maintaining position or status in the conversation.

Report talkers often use language that can be masked as humor but is really meant to be critical.[7] For example, if a report talker arrived at a party and someone else was at the party that they perceived to be some sort of competition, the report talker might say, "Hi Dave, geez, if I knew you were going to be here, I probably would not have come." The statement garners a laugh but is really intended to move the report talker up the social ladder, (I am making fun of you, or simply I am a funny person) and move the recipient (Dave) down the social ladder (You would be the reason I would not attend a function).

Report talk can be very helpful in the right situations. Providing information and knowledge could empower other people to achieve and succeed in a task or situation. Unfortunately, report talk can have a dark side as well. The misuse of report talk could reduce the conversation to a competition or withhold information to abuse power. For example, in a conflict situation, a report talker might choose to sacrifice the relationship if it means they can win the conflict. Sometimes, for a report talker, the only way to maintain position and status is to win at all costs, even if that means hurting or severing the relationship. The report talker might brag, "Well, I won that argument" while the person who was perceived to have lost the argument may no longer want to have anything to do with the perceived winner.

Rapport talkers, on the other hand, see the purpose of language and communication as cultivating, nurturing, and maintaining relationships. Rapport talkers see themselves as individuals in a network of connections. Communication and conversations are negotiations for closeness in which people try to seek and give confirmation and support. Life, then, is about being a member of a community, a struggle to preserve intimacy and avoid isolation.[8] If you ask a rapport talker, "How was your day?" you may get a very long answer. A rapport talker cannot cultivate and nurture a relationship without engaging the other person in their life. This requires a great deal more personal details than just saying, "Fine."

It is not uncommon for rapport talkers to engage in narratives and tell stories. If I ask my wife, "How was your day?" I get a story. My wife might say, "Well, when I first woke up, I could not get out of bed, then when I went into the bathroom, I could not get my contacts in my eyes. Then, I could not find my blue blouse to wear and so I could not wear the outfit I planned to wear. Then, when I went out to the kitchen, someone spilled Cheerios all over the floor and I had to pick that up, then . . .". Sometimes it can take 20 minutes to get me through half of her day! I understand that my wife is a rapport talker; she wants to share her day with me and that means telling me a story that includes many details. Unfortunately, rapport talkers get a bad reputation for talking and telling long stories. This criticism is misdirected. I want the stories from my wife—it means she wants to engage me in her life. I get worried when I ask my wife about her day and she curtly responds, "Fine." That tells me that something is wrong. She does not want to engage me in a story which means she does not want to cultivate our relationship.

In a conflict situation, a rapport talker might sacrifice the conflict to maintain the relationship. Sacrificing the relationship, like a report talker, is not an option for a rapport talker. A rapport talker will often surrender in a conflict (You are right, I was wrong, I am sorry, are we OK?) just so the conflict will go away and the relationship survives. The rapport talker may do this even if they do not believe they are wrong or believe the other person was right. The goal is to maintain the relationship no matter what the cost.

The rapport talker sees themselves as an individual in a circle of people. Communication is the key to connecting everyone in the circle. This means that sometimes a rapport talker will use language that is designed to avoid "telling" another person what they want or think. After a meeting, a rapport talker may say to a coworker, "That was a good meeting, wasn't it?" The phrase "Wasn't it?" is called a tagline and is designed to engage the other person(s) in the conversation. A rapport talker would avoid just saying, "That was a good meeting" because that would not involve others in the conversation. By engaging the phrase, "Wasn't it?" the rapport talker is cultivating and nurturing the relationship by inviting the recipient of the message to share their opinion. The speakers can share their narratives about the meeting and grow in their knowledge of how each other felt, thus maintaining the relationship.

At first glance, report talk may look like the worst option of the two choices. Someone may want to argue that rapport talk is more Christ-like so we should all strive to focus on relationships. However, there are times when report talk is appropriate or the most useful language style for a particular relationship. When the chain of command is imperative in an organization, then report talk is very important. In the military, a commander is more worried about giving an order and having it followed than with how the recipient felt about the order that was given. There are many situations where people with knowledge and expertise need to communicate that information to solve a problem or help individuals learn and grow. Like many teachers, there are times I am asked a question by a student, and rather than give an answer, I engage the Socratic method and respond to the question with another question. Now and then when I respond that way, a student will respond to my question with, "I don't know, that is why I am asking you!" That is also perhaps the reason why you are reading this book, to learn something. You want me to give you information, give you a report, so you can learn from it.

Conversely, while rapport talk may seem like the preferred style of language use, there are times when it may be counterproductive to the relationship. In a coach/athlete relationship, it is far more important that the athlete does what the coach has said than for the coach to worry about how the athlete feels about what has been said. When the coach calls a certain play, that play is to be executed without question or discussion because the coach is supposed to know more than the players, so the players look to the coach for informational language.

From a theoretical perspective, you can see that there is no "one size fits all" approach to language; you must select and choose the style that is appropriate for the situation and that will honor God's gift of language.

James 3:8 and Language

God knew when he gave us the gift of language that the gift had the potential to cause relationship problems. This entire book is about exploring ways to better use your gift of communication by using the lens of Scripture for instructions on how to navigate this difficult topic. There is perhaps no better biblical lens to summarize the challenges of language than James 3:8, where James is very clear on the danger and damage that language can cause by declaring, "But no human being can tame the tongue. It is a restless evil, full of deadly poison."[9] What a bleak warning. Acquired language (the tongue) is called a restless evil and full of deadly poison. James is not the only author in Scripture that warns against the dangers of the tongue. Proverbs 10:19 (NLT) cautions, "Too much talk leads to sin. Be sensible and keep your mouth shut!" And Proverbs 13:3 (NLT) admonishes the reader that, "Those who control their tongue will have a long life; opening your mouth can ruin everything."

Why in the world would God give us *this* gift? The answer is in the first part of James 3:8 where the author instructs us that no human being can tame or control their tongue, only God can do that. This declaration summarizes the challenge of communication that this book is trying to address. My hope is that by understanding how the Bible and our gift of communication are connected, you will finish this book feeling better equipped to handle the challenges that this gift can bring. From a faith perspective, that could mean acknowledging any struggles with language you might have and praying specifically about those needs.

Unwrapping the Languages of Rapport and Report

Many relationships struggle because of the use of rapport versus report talk. It is not uncommon for two people to be in a relationship, even a strong romantic relationship like marriage, and for each person to use a different style. Neither style of language is specific to any gender. A male can use report or rapport and a woman can use report and rapport. A good communicator knows how to adapt their language use and when to use either style. Of the two styles, report talk (maintaining position, power, and status) may seem more prone to representing the perils of the tongue that James 3:8 warns you about, but that does not mean report talk should never be used.

Report talk is not always wrong and can be appropriate in certain situations. However, the drive to maintain position and status can clearly lead to James's description of the tongue containing "deadly poison." The key to using report talk is in the choice of words used to maintain the position and status.

One of the best tools for navigating the use of our gift is awareness of the different communication tools we have at our disposal. When you communicate, you have a choice between report talk or rapport talk, or a mixture of both. God created us to be relational beings, so rapport talk should always be at the forefront of our communication style. However, report talk may be appropriate if you need to give information or knowledge to another person to help or empower them, as long as you use words that honor your gift of communication rather than misuse the gift. Toxic communication, such as making fun of another person, calling a person names, or abusing power through force or verbal abuse should never be an option in your conversations. You are responsible for the language choices you make. You can choose to not speak and stay quiet when needed, and you can choose to not use language that is mean and hurtful. We are responsible for praying about our language and asking for help to make wise choices with the words we use.

5 Ways to Unwrap the Languages of Rapport and Report

1. Understand which language style you prefer—report or rapport. Then, honestly evaluate how you use that style. Make a list of some of the changes you may need to make to your preferred style so that you can avoid the deadly poison that language can create.

2. Make a list of a few of the characteristics of either language style that you may misuse (i.e., heavy use of put-downs). Pray and ask specifically about curtailing the negative use of that characteristic.

3. What are three ways that your tongue can become a *deadly poison*? What specifically can you do to stop using your tongue that way?

4. Pray and ask God to control your tongue. Acknowledge your inability to tame your tongue and understand that only God can do that.

5. Pray for wisdom to understand how to navigate your gift of communication by selecting the best and most appropriate language style to use when you speak.

Conclusion

Language is a by-product of culture. Each culture determines the symbols or words that will make communication possible within that culture. As you move from culture to culture, you must discover the unique language of that culture. I had to learn the differences in language between Southern California and southern Louisiana. You must be aware of the language differences between people as well.

Understanding the difference between report talk and rapport talk is one way to navigate relationships. When you encounter a heavy report talk user, understanding the struggle to maintain position and status can help you avoid being sucked into the dark side of report talk. You can fight the urge to engage in criticism and choose language that adapts to the person but avoids the perils of the tongue. Similarly, when you encounter a rapport-talk person, you can adapt your language use to better cultivate, nurture, and maintain relationships.

Language and communication are gifts from God, but as you are learning in this book, these gifts are rife with perils. Fortunately, God has provided many tools in the Bible to help you navigate how you use your gift. James 3:8 warns about the dangers of language choices and that no person can tame the tongue, only God can do that. If you fail to allow God to control your language choices, the words you speak can become what James described as a "restless evil and a deadly poison." That is a very strong warning that must be heeded for fear that you may fall victim to the dark side of communication and find yourself misusing your gift.

• Prayer Prompt •

Father, thank you for your gift of communication. Thank you for the different approaches to communication that we have and how we can build relationships with our gift. Forgive me when I have not tamed my tongue and forgive me for when I have let the deadly poison of my language choices be released through my words. I pray for wisdom to see the difference between my language choices and the courage to make the right choice and choose the most appropriate style that honors you. I ask for courage to choose to stop using language characteristics that are hurtful and mean and do not honor you. In Jesus's name, Amen.

Chapter 6: Follow-Up Questions

1. Which style of language resonates with you the most—report or rapport? Are you attached to one style or do you think you can learn both? Why or why not?

2. Do you have any relationships or situations in your life that need or require report talk? Who are those relationship(s) with and how do you navigate them?

3. Do you have any relationships in your life that need or require rapport talk? Who are those relationships with and how do you navigate them?

4. What characteristics of each language choice are appealing to you? What are some ways you may have misused those characteristics? What can you do to address that misuse?

5. James 3:8 warns us that no human being can control their tongue. Does that verse give you hope or discourage you? Explain your answer.

Chapter 7

Please Wash My Feet!

Nonverbal Communication, Expectancy Violations Theory, and John 13:1–17

If you expect nothing from somebody you are never disappointed.[1]
—Sylvia Plath

When you stop expecting people to be perfect, you can like them for who they are.[2]

—Donald Miller

SEVERAL YEARS AGO, I TAUGHT at a university with a colleague who took a unique approach to the first day of each semester in his public speaking classes. To better understand this story, allow me to provide you with some context and background.

We were both teaching at a small, private, somewhat conservative college in the Midwest. Diversity was not a strength of the college, so, on the first day of classes, my colleague would walk into class dressed like a stereotypical motorcycle gang member. He would wear big biker boots, black leather pants, torn black t-shirt, black leather vest with motorcycle club patches all over it, and he topped it all off with the requisite bandana and sunglasses. He arrived late to class on purpose to make a grand entrance and be seen by everyone in the room. He would proceed with the usual first-day-of-class information (syllabi, course expectations, attendance policy, etc.) by talking as if he were in a motorcycle gang complete with profanity and intimidating glares at students over the top of his sunglasses if anyone laughed or failed to respond the way he wanted them to.

I enjoyed hearing the accounts of his first day in these classes. Some students loved his presentation thinking, "Wow, finally a cool professor!"

Some students would laugh and see his attire as a joke. But some students were terribly confused and did not have a clue what to think of the entire situation. Some of those students would immediately walk to the Registrar's Office to drop the class.[3] Whatever the reaction from the students, he would achieve his goal, which was to get them thinking. For the second and subsequent classes, he would arrive dressed in his normal teaching clothes which included a conservative suit and tie.

When he walked into class dressed in a suit, he generated more confusion in the students' minds. He would then engage the class in a discussion about communication expectations, credibility, integrity, nonverbal communication, and how a person's expectations shape how a message is received. The discussion allowed him to engage in an explanation of how the students arrived in class expecting a college professor, which meant that each student came to class with some sort of preconceived idea and expectation of how a college professor at a small, private conservative school should look and act. When that expectation (professor in a suit) was violated (person in motorcycle gang clothes) it created a great deal of confusion for some students, especially those who ran to drop the class.

The entire activity and subsequent class discussions laid an excellent foundation for my colleague to begin by showing the students the many different variables (like expectations) that can unknowingly create prejudicial barriers in our communication transactions. He was able to expand the example to topics such as what kind of expectations we place on communication transactions with parents, family, friends, significant others, people of faith, people who profess no faith, professors, waitstaff at restaurants, retail clerks, and on and on. Whether the students liked it or not, my colleague was very successful in showing and teaching about the different barriers we carry with us into every communication transaction and how those expectations can sometimes be violated and adversely affect the communication process. This process of responding to preconceived communication expectations is the focus of Expectancy Violations Theory (EVT). This chapter will explore the theoretical lens of EVT and the insights it offers for relational communication, see what the Bible teaches about the phenomenon of expectations being violated, and finally, provide some guidelines for healthy nonverbal communication patterns.

Expectancy Violations Theory

EVT identifies how we hold certain expectations for behavior by other people.[4] Originally designed to explain nonverbal behavior between people, EVT has grown to encompass a wide range of behavioral expectations.[5] The study of EVT includes the way messages are presented to others and the types of behaviors undertaken during a conversation. The expectations that people hold regarding what is considered appropriate nonverbal behaviors in society have been found to drive communication transactions. For example, when you greet someone in certain cultures, it is considered appropriate to use a firm handshake with direct eye contact. However, in some countries, the traditional form of greeting is a bow, with the depth and length of the bow conveying differing meanings in cultural status.[6] Whatever form of greeting is expected in a particular culture, when two people greet each other, and one of them does not engage in the expected behavior, violating that expectation draws attention. The attention to the violation can create tension in the relationship that one, or both, individuals may feel the need to resolve.

My colleague arriving for the first day of class looking like a motorcycle gang member violated the students' expectations of a professor. This violation of the expected norm created tension for the students. Some students resolved the tension by thinking about how cool he was and accepted the violation. Some students resolved the tension by assuming it was some sort of a joke, and some students resolved the tension by trying to drop the class. The communication process for each student involved interpreting the message through their filters and past experiences. In Chapter 2, we saw how the only message that counts is the message received because that is the message the receiver will respond to. Receivers of messages are going to respond to an expected violation based on their interpretation of the violation/message (cool professor, some sort of joke, or unacceptable behavior and I'm dropping the class).

Certain expectations become societal norms and stereotypes. EVT asserts that these expected behaviors are learned. People in the United States are not born with an automatic tendency to shake hands, they usually must be taught that this is the appropriate and expected greeting. Conversely, people in other countries are not born with an automatic tendency to bow, the behavior must be learned. As members of a culture learn the expected behaviors of that culture, they learn that these behaviors are societal norms that cultures expect when interacting with people in various situations.

Furthermore, EVT proposes that when a violation of an expectation occurs, attention is drawn to that violation. Less attention is paid to the message the other person is trying to communicate and more attention is given to the behavior that violated expectations. The attention, or arousal, to the violation can be both cognitive and physical. With cognitive arousal, our intuitive sense is heightened, and we are aware that a violation occurred. Physical arousal includes such responses as elevated heart rate, increased pulse volume, and raised skin temperature. Whatever the form of arousal, the affected person's response to it is determined by what EVT scholars refer to as a "threat threshold"[7] which is how much tolerance there is for the violation. The greater the physical and psychological discomfort a person experiences when an expectation is violated, the more likely it is to make them feel threatened. Their interpretation of the other person's intentions is another factor determining whether the threat threshold is reached and how they respond. They may respond to the threat with a social reward (such as admiration or laughter), overlooking/excusing the behavior, or punishment based on their assessment of the violation as a creative/teaching moment, a joke, an honest mistake, or a deliberately offensive act. For the students in my colleague's first day of classes who ran to the Registrar's Office to drop the class, they clearly reached their threat threshold. They expected a competent professor of good character never to behave in such a manner.

As EVT shows, assessing the violator's knowledge and intentions allows us to decide how to respond to an expectancy violation. A few years ago, I traveled to several south-east Asian countries. It is customary in the countries I visited to hand your money or credit card to a cashier or business owner by holding it with both hands and extending the money or card to the cashier at about waist level. I tried my best to remember to pay for things that way as a sign of respect for the cultural expectation. However, since it was a new behavior for me, I forgot several times. My mistake was often overlooked and greeted with kindness and my payment was taken from me. However, on a few occasions, the recipient of my money exchange would bow their head and stand and wait for me to hand my money to them correctly. EVT explains how and why some people excused my error, while others preferred that I adhered to the expectation.

John 13:1–17: Jesus Washes the Disciples' Feet

Jesus was well known for challenging expected (or normal) behavior. He ate with sinners,[8] hung out with rich, questionable people,[9] healed the sick on the Sabbath,[10] raised the dead,[11] and picked and ate food on the Sabbath.[12] One of his biggest "violations" of normal behavior took place on the eve of his betrayal and crucifixion when he washed the feet of his disciples. John 13:1–17 recorded the event:

> It was just before the Passover Festival. Jesus knew that the hour had come for him to leave this world and go to the Father. Having loved his own who were in the world, he loved them to the end.
>
> The evening meal was in progress, and the devil had already prompted Judas, the son of Simon Iscariot, to betray Jesus. Jesus knew that the Father had put all things under his power, and that he had come from God and was returning to God; so he got up from the meal, took off his outer clothing, and wrapped a towel around his waist. After that, he poured water into a basin and began to wash his disciples' feet, drying them with the towel that was wrapped around him.
>
> He came to Simon Peter, who said to him, "Lord, are you going to wash my feet?"
>
> Jesus replied, "You do not realize now what I am doing, but later you will understand."
>
> "No," said Peter, "you shall never wash my feet."
>
> Jesus answered, "Unless I wash you, you have no part with me."
>
> "Then, Lord," Simon Peter replied, "not just my feet but my hands and my head as well!"
>
> Jesus answered, "Those who have had a bath need only to wash their feet; their whole body is clean. And you are clean, though not every one of you." For he knew who was going to betray him, and that was why he said not everyone was clean.
>
> When he had finished washing their feet, he put on his clothes and returned to his place. "Do you understand what I have done for you?" he asked them. "You call me 'Teacher' and 'Lord,' and rightly so, for that is what I am. Now that I, your Lord and Teacher, have washed your feet, you also should wash one another's feet. I have set you an example that you should do as I have done for

you. Very truly I tell you, no servant is greater than his master, nor is a messenger greater than the one who sent him.

Now that you know these things, you will be blessed if you do them."

In that culture, washing a person's feet was considered a menial task usually done by servants and not something to be done by a religious teacher or authority, and certainly not the Messiah.[13] Peter provided a glimpse into how inappropriate it was for Jesus to wash the disciples' feet in verse eight when he exclaimed, "You shall never wash my feet!" Jesus violated both the expectations of the culture (by doing a servant's task) and the disciples' expectations for the Messiah (The Messiah should never do something this menial). The violation created tension for Peter, and he sought to relieve that tension by exclaiming that Jesus would never wash his feet.

However, Jesus responded to Peter by declaring that foot washing was required if Peter wanted to be a part of Jesus. Impetuous Peter desired so much to be a part of Jesus that he blurted out his response, "Not just my feet but my hands and my head as well." This declaration, however impetuous or misguided, provided Peter the resolution to the tension that Jesus's act of foot washing created in violation of the cultural expectation regarding a job reserved for servants. Jesus expanded his response in the subsequent verses and explained that he was washing their feet as an example of how he wanted the disciples to act towards one another and the world. The biblical lens calling the disciples to take on the role of a servant was a metaphor for humility. Jesus concluded by promising the disciples that they would be blessed when they acted toward others with this same type of humility.

Unwrapping the Gift of Communication in Response to Expectancy Violations

A few years ago, I was talking with a couple at a retreat I was speaking at, and they were sharing with me some of the communication challenges they were experiencing. It seemed that there were times when the husband would say or do something that was hurtful or upsetting to the wife. She would respond by not communicating with him (usually nonverbally—i.e., by not talking to him). When he would ask her what was wrong, she would attack him and say "I shouldn't have to tell you. You should know what you did!" The man would usually not have a clue what was wrong and when he would press his wife for an explanation, she would respond, "If you really loved me, you should know." When I asked the wife, "Why should he know?" she could only say "Because he says he loves me."

It was clear to me that the wife had a very clear expectation of what it meant to love someone (to be able to read their mind) and a clear expectation of how her husband should communicate with her. To the wife, if someone loved her, it meant that they should know when they have hurt or wronged her. Obviously, that is not always possible. I know my wife's strengths and weaknesses and I know to avoid saying certain words that can hurt her. But even though I know her trigger words, it does not mean that I never make a mistake and never say or do something hurtful. Sometimes I say something hurtful and do not even realize that I made a mistake. In those times, my wife must be transparent and tell me, "When you said/ did this, it hurt my feelings." Only then can I clearly know what I did wrong, and I can apologize and try to right the wrong.

The problem for the couple I was talking with at the retreat was that the wife had never spelled out for the husband what she expected from him regarding his behavior. The wife had an expectation of what a husband should do and when that expectation was violated it affected how the couple communicated. Whenever you project an expectation into a relationship, yet never clearly communicate that expectation to the other person, that person is eventually going to fail to meet your expectation.

The expectations we place on communication transactions reach beyond just husbands and wives. I have seen customers in a restaurant get angry with a waitstaff person because they did not greet them when they entered the restaurant or did not take their order the way the customer felt it should be taken. The expectation (a waitstaff person should act a certain way) was violated (the waitstaff person did not act in the expected way) which created tension for the customer, which is communicated through anger or some other form of negative message. I have had students get upset with me when they ask me a question and I do not give them a specific answer. I might try a Socratic method approach and answer their question with another question. They will tell me, "I don't know, that's why I'm asking you!" The student brought an expectation into our communication transaction—"We, the students, ask you, the professor questions, and then you, the professor, give us an answer to that question." When that exchange does not happen, the expectation is violated, and the tension of the violation affects our communication.

Think for a minute of the expectations you place on the people in your life—friends, family, significant others, spouses, even retail clerks—how do those expectations affect your communication interactions with those people? Do you find yourself getting frustrated or angry with someone because they violated an unknown expectation? Keep in mind, I am not saying it is OK for people (especially husbands and wives) to intentionally go around saying or doing mean things and then blame it on failed expectations. In Chapter 6, I explored the role of responsibility and accountability in your use of language. But do you find yourself getting short with people because they did not respond or act the way you wanted them to? I recently had one of my children express to me how upset they were with someone because they reached out to them, and the other person did not respond the way my child wanted them to respond. They told me, "I would never act like that so why would they?" The answer was simple—because they are not you.

It is not wrong to have expectations. It is common to teach children to say "please" and "thank you." I taught my children to always greet people with a smile and a firm handshake. In school, children are taught to raise their hand and wait their turn to be called on to speak rather than just speaking out loud and everyone talking at the same time. All cultures have their own set of reasonable expectations regarding communication. You may even have your own set of expectations that differ from the types of behaviors you find acceptable and comfortable in the daily cultures you experience. From the theoretical perspective of EVT, it is important to understand why and how you respond to perceived violations. Do you lash out in anger, or do you pause and consider what expected violations may be driving your anger? From the faith perspective given to us in John 13, we can also see that sometimes God violates our expectations to teach us an important lesson—and Jesus might even do this through people who do not behave as we expect. This reminds us that we should not respond to expectancy violations with a knee-jerk reaction; we need to reflect on what is happening and what we can learn from it—like the students who stayed in my colleague's classroom.

5 Ways to Unwrap How You Navigate Expectancy Violations

1. Realize the human tendency to place communication expectations on other people. It is normal but needs to be kept in check. Are you being fair to the people you are placing the expectations on?

2. Make sure you are differentiating between acceptable cultural expectations (i.e., "please" and "thank you," shaking hands, etc.) and your own expectations. Are you placing expectations on other people to promote your own selfishness just to be critical of others?

3. Stop using your communication expectations as an excuse to be angry, mean, or critical of other people. That is misusing your gift of communication for selfish reasons and does not honor God.

4. Pray and ask God to show you where you might be placing unrealistic or unfair expectations on other people. For example, expecting a romantic partner to "read your mind" is not fair to them.

5. Make sure you have clearly expressed your communication expectations to people who are very close and important to you. It is the people who are closest to you that can cause the most hurt.

Conclusion

I have never entered a classroom on the first day of class dressed in a motorcycle gang outfit, but I have projected unrealistic and unfair expectations on other people for many different reasons. I have had to intentionally change how I communicate with other people to use my gift of communication to honor God and not promote my selfishness. Expectancy Violations Theory sheds some light on what happens when your communication expectations are violated and how you react to that violation. Understanding the communication process and the choices you make when you feel that a violation has taken place allows you to stop and think before you respond. Jesus violated the disciples' expectations by humbling himself to wash their feet, an act of the lowest servant, so they could gain a new understanding of God's loving heart and learn to serve one another in love, as he did.

• Prayer Prompt •

Heavenly Father, thank you for your gift of communication. I am very grateful for this gift you have trusted me with. Forgive me when I have misused your gift, especially when I have placed expectations on other people that have not been fair or justified. Give me the words I need to clearly express my expectations to those people who are closest to me. In Jesus's name, Amen.

Chapter 7: Follow-Up Questions

1. What sort of communication expectations do you place on people around you? Do people with different roles in your life get different expectations? What are some of those communication expectations?

2. How are your communication expectations different with a romantic partner than with just a friend? Does your partner know your expectations? How can you communicate those expectations to them?

3. Do you get angry at a person who violates your communication expectations? Why do you think you get angry?

4. Have you ever had inappropriate or unreasonable communication expectations placed upon you by another person? Who was the person and what was the expectation? Were you able to resolve the tension caused by the incorrect expectation? Why or why not?

5. Have you ever experienced a foot-washing experience like the story of Jesus and his disciples presented in John 13:1–17? Were you the giver or the receiver of the foot washing (or both)? Describe the experience.

Chapter 8

Do You Hear What I Hear?

The Gift of Listening and John 11:41–42

We have been given two ears and but a single mouth, in order that we may hear more and talk less.[1]

—Greek Philosopher

MANY YEARS AGO, I WAS A YOUTH PASTOR at a church in Southern California. A popular icebreaker game we used to play in both the junior high and high school groups was called "telephone." Perhaps you have played this game where one person begins by whispering a specific message into a second person's ear. The message can be a long thought, a quotation, or a brief story. The second person repeats the message to a third person, who passes the message on to a fourth person, and so on until the entire group has shared the message. The last person to receive the message announces to the entire group what they believe is the message being shared. The leader of the group then reads the original message shared by the first person in the chain and, without fail, the final message shared, and the original message read, are rarely close. While this game is a fun icebreaker and good for some innocent laughs, the game requires excellent listening skills and illustrates just how difficult listening can be.

Even if you have never played "telephone," I am willing to bet you have experienced a listening breakdown of some shape, manner, or form. Everyone has experienced the communication breakdown I identified previously in Chapter 2 of a listener hearing and interpreting a message incorrectly (shots versus socks) and responding poorly. Something so simple—letting sound waves bounce off our eardrums—can be catastrophic.

Poor listening can cause so many problems in a relationship that some relationships cannot survive the problem. How does this happen? And why does it happen so often? The answer to these questions can be found in understanding God's purpose and plan for the gift of listening as part of our gift of communication. Failed relationships because of poor listening do not honor God. I have heard so many couples complain to me, "We'd get along so much better if he would just listen to me," or "I feel she never listens to me or cares about what I have to say." Those kinds of struggles are not what good communication is about or the reason why God gave us the ability to listen. This chapter will explore listening by looking at what God has to say about listening in the Bible, then exploring some simple steps you can take to become a better listener.

John 11:41–42: God Listens to Us

When confronted with the task of answering the question, "Why should I listen?" it does not take long to find a biblical lens to answer that question. The Bible is filled with references to God listening and hearing people who pray or cry out to him (for example Exodus 2:23–24 or Psalm 6:8–9). But it is not just people in the Bible who identify that God listens; even Jesus, when he was on earth as a human being, knew that he could count on God to listen to him. John 11:41–42 highlighted Jesus's mindset by stating, "And Jesus lifted His eyes and said, 'Father, I thank thee that thou hast heard me. And I know that thou hast heard me always." In this passage, we read about Jesus raising Lazarus from the dead. Before Jesus performed this miracle, he publicly prayed and spoke to God so all those who could hear him would know that it was God who was at work doing this miracle. Jesus had no reservations that God was listening to his prayers for this miracle, and he acknowledged his confidence that God was always listening to him.

Scripture reinforces one of the foundational beliefs of people of faith that God listens to us. If people of faith did not believe that God listens, then why bother to pray? When you pray, you do so from the presupposition that God is listening and that he hears your prayers. God's providence dictates the answer to the prayer, but you must have zero reservations about the prayer being heard.

Reflect on Chapter 2 and the reference to James 1:19 where Christians are called to emulate the God who listens. People of faith are to be quick to listen, slow to speak, and slow to anger. Just as you expect God to listen to you, God expects you to listen to others.

Another foundational premise of being a person of faith is found in 1 John 4:8, "Whoever does not love does not know God, because God is love."

There are several references in Scripture identifying God as synonymous with love (John 5:42, 2 Cor. 13:11, 1 John 4:7). This becomes another foundational belief for people of faith.

From a faith perspective, these two foundational beliefs set the stage for a syllogistic answer to the question of why you should be a good listener. I would argue that, if "God is love" (a foundational faith belief), and "God listens" (evident throughout Scripture), then "listening is loving." In Scripture we are commanded to love one another. John 15:12 notes, "My commandment is this: Love each other as I have loved you." I do not know about you, but I have some people in my life that are hard to love. I wish God gave me an out in Scripture like, "Love most people," or "Love everyone you get along with." But unfortunately, he did not. God commanded you to love everyone just as he loves you. How can you do this when it seems so hard? I have found that since God loves me, and God listens, then when I learn how to simply listen to others, I am loving them the way God loves me. For the people in my life that are hard to love, I set a goal to just listen to them. I tell God that I find it hard to love some people, so I will just listen to them. God tells me, "That is fine, I can love them through you if you will just show them my love by listening."

Unwrapping Good Listening Skills

It is easy to say, "Be a good listener." The problem is that if I ask ten people to define what it means to be a good listener, I get ten different answers. Part of the difficulty in defining listening lies in the fact that listening is not a single act. In fact, most scholars define listening as a "process" that involves multiple stages.[2] To be a good listener and love others the way that God loves you, you need to understand the listening process and use some specific tools to navigate that process.

I propose five steps to use to become a better listener. First, ask questions. A good listener knows that when a person speaks, they may have trouble articulating what is on their mind. Often, a person may not know how to express their thoughts or ideas, so they struggle to clearly explain themselves. Sometimes, a person may think they are clearly communicating their thoughts only to find out they are failing miserably. Also, remember Chapter 2 and the six elements all messages include? What a person wants to say and what they do say, can often be two different things, or the interpretation of the message received by the listener can be incorrect. By asking questions, the listener can clarify the feelings, the emotions, the situation, or the context of what is being said. Recently, I had a young woman tell me, "My boyfriend is driving me crazy!" That was a very broad and vague statement. I had no idea what it was that the boyfriend was doing that was driving her so crazy. Everybody is different when it comes to things people do that can irritate them, and what might drive this woman crazy might not bother me at all. So, I started asking her some questions. "What does he do that drives you crazy?" She explained, "He is always late. He says he will pick me up at seven o'clock but then does not show up until an hour later at eight o'clock. This has happened several times!" I now had a specific action by the boyfriend that I could address. The boyfriend's behavior that was bothering her was his tardiness.

A good rule to follow for asking questions is to try and avoid closed questions—those questions that can be answered with a simple yes or no. These types of questions tend to repress conversations and shut down dialogue. Rather than ask a person, "Are you happy?" ask, "Tell me three things that make you happy." Another helpful question-asking guideline is to follow the basic five Ws and one H—Who, What, When, Where, Why, and How. Again, rather than ask a person "Are you happy?" focus on "Who makes you happy?" "What types of things make you happy?" "When were times in your life when you were happy?" "Where are some places where you feel happiest?" "Why did those times, or those places make you happy?" And "How do you seek out happiness?" These types of questions can foster conversation and suggest follow-up questions that a good listener can ask.

The second step to being a good listener is to seek specifics. By asking questions, it allows you, as the listener, to probe deeper and find out what is going on. The more questions you ask, the closer you can get to understanding the core of the problem. Often, the problem named by the person is not the real problem at all. With the student who told me her boyfriend was driving her crazy, rather than just reacting to the "driving me crazy" statement, I found out the problem had to do with his tardiness. But even with that knowledge, I still did not know all the details. I asked another question, "Have you told him that his tardiness bothers you?" She replied, "No, I do not want to cause an argument." I responded, "What do you do when he arrives late?" She explained, "I try to just smile and pretend it does not bother me. Once or twice, I tried to drop a hint by saying 'I hope we aren't late to the movie/party we are going to.'" I probed, "What did he say to those hints?" "He laughed and shrugged and did not seem to care." I pressed her, "Do you think he cares?" She responded, "No, because how can he say he loves me yet not care enough to keep his word so I can trust what he says? How can our relationship grow and get serious when I can never trust him? I really care about him, but I cannot be in a long-term relationship without any trust." That was a great eye-opening piece of information for me. I pressed further, "Do you see yourself wanting to be in a long-term relationship with him, possibly leading to marriage?" She paused, then said, "Yes, he has many of the qualities I am looking for in someone." I queried, "Do you think he is interested in a long-term relationship as well?" She blurted out, "How can he when he treats me like this? I feel the relationship is too one-sided. He is not putting as much effort into the relationship as I am."

By continuing to ask questions based on her answers to my previous questions, I was able to get more to the root of the problem. She was struggling with trust in the relationship based on her boyfriend's constant tardiness. By asking questions, I was able to discover that she was afraid of where things were headed. She wanted a long-term relationship but saw his tardiness as a sign that he was not as committed to her as she was to him. She also revealed that she had never spoken to him directly about her feelings (which was a separate problem in itself). This encompassed failed expectations, as covered in Chapter 7 of this book. I now had much more information to explore with her.

After asking questions, and seeking specifics, the third step to being a good listener is to paraphrase what you hear. Paraphrasing is the process of restating back to the other person, in your own words, what you think you heard them say.[3] This allows you to make sure you are responding to the real root of the problem rather than just the first words you heard. This may often be done by simply saying phrases such as, "What I hear you saying is . . .", "It sounds like you are saying . . .", or "It sounds like you feel . . .". It is important that paraphrasing creates an opportunity for the other person to correct you. Sometimes it is good to follow up a paraphrased statement with, "Am I hearing you correctly?" or "Did I get that gist of what you are saying?"

Paraphrasing can also go both ways. Sometimes when I am talking to someone, I will ask them, "Tell me what you hear me saying." This allows me to check and see if I am clearly communicating what I want to say to the person who is listening to me. Remember the six elements all messages go through? Paraphrasing allows you to keep the conversation on track and avoid having two different conversations. If I had only responded to the student's original comment about being driven crazy, I would only offer her comfort for that single emotion, but that emotion was not the core of the problem. She was very afraid of where the relationship was headed based on her boyfriend's tardiness.

When the woman told me her boyfriend was driving her crazy, I could have just replied, "I'm sorry. Boyfriends will do that!" But that response does very little to address the student's real fear, which had to do with long-term marriage ideas. After asking questions, I was able to paraphrase my thoughts and say, "What I hear you saying is that you are afraid that his tardiness is a sign that he does not respect you and that scares you." She started crying and said, "Yes, how did you know?"

In the fourth step to good listening, the listener knows to avoid evaluative statements. It is best if you avoid telling another person how to feel. To the other person, their feelings are real and valid, and the emotion is present for a reason. Even if the reason is illogical, misguided, or off base to you, the feeling is still very real to the other person. A good listener knows this and always tries to avoid telling the person how to feel or making an evaluative statement. Statements such as "Don't be angry," "There's no need to feel that way," "Why are you so upset?" or "That's silly to feel that way" are evaluations. These types of statements only serve to make the other person defensive because they feel the need to protect their feelings, or they feel criticized for feeling a certain way that is justified by something that was said or done toward them. It can also be very helpful to try and avoid "why" questions such as, "Why did you do that?" "Why does that bother you so much?" or "Why do you not want to go?" While the word "why" may seem like the right way to collect more information, the word can trigger a negative or defensive response in the speaker. If the speaker is already feeling defensive, they may hear "why" as questioning their judgment or character, even if the questioner was simply asking an innocent question. You may find it helpful to have some alternative words ready to use instead of why. Sometimes asking "What led you to feel that way?" or "What were the chain of events leading up to your situation?" can set a more exploratory tone to the conversation rather than a critical one. When my children make a choice or a decision that I do not understand, rather than asking, "Why did you do that?" which can sound very accusatory, I have had a great deal of success with asking, "Walk me through your thinking on how you made that decision." This type of statement can seem much more investigative than accusatory.

The admonition to avoid evaluative statements does not mean that you always must agree with the person you are listening to. In your mind you might think, "That is silly to be upset with someone who is tardy," but saying that thought will not make you a good listener. A good listener knows to support the emotion you are hearing the other person communicate. A good listener would respond with, "You sound like you are really upset with your boyfriend's tardiness." These types of non-evaluative statements allow a good listener to validate the emotions they hear in the message from the other person, which allows the listener to just love the person who is sharing.

The fifth and final step to being a good listener is not to offer advice unless asked. I think one of the biggest mistakes in listening is we tend to think the only reason someone is telling us something is to get our advice. That is a very self-centered reaction. Author Stephen Covey notes, "Most people do not listen with the intent to understand; they listen with the intent to reply."[4] Remember back in Chapter 6 and the use of Report talk: When listening to someone else, a report talker is tempted to build up their value and status in the conversation by talking about what they know or what they would do. They may think they are just trying to help and be oblivious to the ways in which giving makes them feel important. Sometimes being a good listener means being able to be a Rapport talker—listening to build rapport, to focus on the relationship, not on solutions. Sometimes a person just needs to tell someone something to get it off their chest. I call it "verbally vomiting." Some days I come home from work and my wife will ask me how my day was. When I tell her, "I need to verbally vomit for a while," she knows I just need to vent and talk and express some things that are on my mind without any input or reflection. It is when I tell my wife, "Tell me what you would do if this happened to you…" she knows that I am open to her advice.

You might be thinking, "But I know exactly what that person is feeling and going through, I have the answer for them!" That is true, you might. But if they have not asked you for your advice, there is a good chance your words will fall on closed ears. Our pride makes us want to stop listening and just start talking and giving advice. Our ego gets in the way of being a good listener. God is very clear in Scripture on how he feels about our pride (e.g., Proverbs 6:16). To be a good listener means putting your pride in check and fighting the urge to always give advice, thinking you know it all. A good listener knows to always put the other person first, to love them as we have been commanded. If listening is loving, then listening means not offering advice.

That seems to be a little bit like how God listens to us. I have often gone to God and just needed to vent and spew and get things off my mind. I imagine God listening to me vent and just smiling and nodding, waiting for me to ask him, "OK, God, what do you think I should do?" God replies, "Well, now that you ask, here is what I already gave you in my Word . . ."

If you do feel the need to offer your advice, remember that the fifth step is not to offer advice unless asked. One way you can test the waters and see if the person you are listening to is open to any advice is to simply ask them. When the young woman was telling me her boyfriend was driving her crazy, after I asked several questions, I first validated the emotion I heard and said "Wow, you sound really upset by this. Is there anything I can do to help?" She smiled and said, "No, not really, I just needed to talk to someone. So, thank you for listening." Inside my mind, I was thinking, "But I know what you need to do to fix this." However, she just told me she did not want my advice, so for me to push it and try to tell her how to fix her problem would just be my pride trying to force my beliefs and ideas onto her. That is not how God listens to us and it is not how we should listen to other people. God gives us free will to ask him for advice or choose not to listen to him. If I ask a person, "How can I help?" and they respond, "Well, what would you do in my situation?" then they have opened the door and asked for my advice. They are now open and willing to listen to what I want to share. It is a little like how I imagine God listens to us. God knows what is right and best for us, he just waits for us to say, "God, what do you want?" and he is ready to let us know. But if I ask a person, "How can I help you?" and they respond, "You don't need to. Thanks for listening," they have communicated they are not open to listening to me.

A good listener knows how pride can take over and ruin a listening opportunity. It is very tempting to want to listen by talking. We want to fix problems, we want to know all the answers, and we want to talk and tell the other person what to do. That is talking, not listening, and that talking is driven by pride that God hates. A good listener knows to check their pride at the door and follow the five steps to good listening. From a theoretical lens, a good listener also knows that it is not easy to listen well, and it takes strength to put our pride and ego aside to listen. Communication expert Quentin Schultze notes, "Many people lack the courage to listen to others without scrutinizing them."[5] Our pride wants to scrutinize other people, to show them where and why they are wrong. We do that because it makes us feel better about ourselves. It takes courage to close our mouths and not judge, critique, or scrutinize someone. It takes courage to be a good listener.

One way to learn and remember these five steps to good listening is to put them on a notecard and tape it to your bathroom or dresser mirror or wherever you know you will see it every day. Pray and ask the Lord to help you live out these steps and to check your pride at the door and make an honest effort to become the type of person who loves by truly listening to the other person.

5 Ways to Unwrap the Gift of Listening

1. Ask Open Questions: Avoid closed questions that can be answered with a "yes" or "no." Remember, the first words out of a person's mouth are often not what the real problem is all about. Asking questions allows you to unwrap the problem and find out what is really going on.

2. Seek Specifics: Ask follow-up questions based on your initial questions to keep probing and going deeper to find the root of the matter.

3. Paraphrase What You Hear: Repeat back to the other person, in your own words, what you hear them saying. Get their feedback and approval. Keep your interpretation of the message on track so you avoid having two different conversations. And remember, paraphrasing goes both ways. If you are the one sharing, you can ask the other person to paraphrase back to you what they hear you saying.

4. Avoid Evaluative Statements: Never criticize a person's emotions or what they share they are feeling. Those emotions are real to that person and a good listener knows to support the emotion, even if the listener disagrees with the emotion.

5. Do Not Offer Advice Unless Asked: Fight the urge to talk and give answers. That is your pride at work. Listening is loving so do not offer your advice unless the person asks for it. You can always ask someone "How can I help" and they will communicate to you that they are either open or not interested in your advice based on how they answer.

Conclusion

Not every listening situation has to be as challenging or as difficult as the "telephone" game. However, good listening is intentional and takes effort. You must make a conscious effort to be a good listener; it does not come as naturally as you might think or hope.

As a person of faith, I believe that God listens to my prayers. I also firmly believe that God is love. Based on those beliefs, I argue that listening is loving. God commanded me to love others, even when they are unlovable. One way to love the unlovable is to just listen to them. Let God love them through you by your listening skills. God calls you to love everyone, so you not only need to love the unlovable by listening, you need to make sure you are loving those close to you in a way that honors God—by truly listening, not just to their words, but to the emotions behind the words. God gave you two ears and one mouth for a reason, as Zeno noted, *so that you can hear more and talk less.*

• Prayer Prompt •

Father, thank you for your gift of communication. Thank you for giving me the gift of listening as well. You command me to love others, and one of the biggest ways I can love someone is to just listen to them—like you are listening to me now. How easy it is to take listening for granted. Forgive me for the times I have failed to listen to those around me, meaning I have failed to love them. Forgive me for taking for granted the way you listen to me, even when I am complaining and rambling on. Help me check my pride at the door. I ask for the ability to remember and practice the five steps to being a good listener. In Jesus's name, Amen.

Chapter 8: Follow-Up Questions

1. Who in your life do you consider to be a good listener? What is it about that person that makes them a good listener for you?

2. Do you believe that God is love? Do you believe that God listens? Do you believe that listening is loving? Why or why not?

3. Who are some people in your life that you find hard to love? Is there

a way you can love them by listening to them? What might that look like?

4. Which of the five steps to better listening is easy for you (if any)? What makes it easy for you?

5. Which of the five steps to better listening seems the hardest for you to follow? Why will that one be the hardest? What can you do to try to make it an easier step to follow?

Chapter 9

Let's Make a Deal!

Social Exchange Theory and Mark 10:17–22

What good will it be for someone to gain the whole world, yet forfeit their soul? Or what can anyone give in exchange for their soul?

—Matthew 16:26

Surround yourself with only people who are going to lift you higher.[1]

—Oprah Winfrey

As a child growing up in the 1960s, I had the opportunity to experience television in its early days. Through the years, television shows have morphed and grown into the programs we have today, for better or for worse. One staple of daytime television through the years has been game shows. As a child, I was addicted to *Let's Make A Deal* with host Monty Hall. I would fake being sick so I could stay home from school and watch Monty give away the Big Deal of the Day as long as the lucky contestant avoided getting "Zonked!" The show has been revived today but the premise remains the same. A contestant often must choose between $1000 cash or what is behind door number one. Door number one could reveal a new car or a "Zonk"—a stuffed panda bear. It would cost the contestant $1000 to see what is behind the door. The contestant must decide if the risk is worth the chance to get a better reward. Sometimes the contestant gets a new car and sometimes they get a stuffed panda bear.

Relationships with people can be just like *Let's Make a Deal*. We seek out and need relationships as a natural part of being human, but all relationships carry a cost. We want the reward (a new car) but are often afraid of the cost (giving up $1000). We want friends and companions (reward) but can be afraid of rejection and hurt (cost). It is easy to be disappointed in relationships and get hurt. That is why it is helpful to have tools and guidelines to help us weigh out the risks and costs of relationships.

All relationships cost you something—time, money, choices, power. Even a simple relationship between you and a salesperson requires you to self-disclose what you need. When you walk into a store, the salesperson has no idea what you specifically need until you tell them. This level of cost is usually not very problematic. We engage in sharing information about ourselves ("I need to find a suit") because the reward (getting a new suit) is what we are looking for.

When it comes to friendships or romantic relationships, the cost is far greater. Sharing information about yourself is a normal part of life. Who has not joined a new group and had to go around and share your favorite color, favorite movie, or favorite musician/song/album? For some people, this type of activity is fun and enjoyable, but for others, this type of activity can be very hard. Sharing information about yourself (a cost) is not something you take lightly or enjoy (a low reward).

There is an old saying, "Information is power." When you share information about yourself with another person, it gives that person a little bit of power over you—they know some things about you. This power becomes threatening if the person you share the information with rejects the information or makes fun of something you share. If I tell you, "I like the music group U2," and you laugh and respond, "They are horrible. How could you like them?!"—that is rejection which is very powerful because rejection hurts. If I want to avoid rejection (and hurt) I will choose to not answer a question, so I do not give you any possible power over me.

Not all sharing is bad or negative. In fact, sharing and exchanging information is how you get to know other people and build relationships, and everyone needs relationships. God made you to be a relational being. When you share information about yourself with another person, it creates a connection, especially when you discover things that you have in common with the other person. The more things you discover that you have in common with another person, the stronger the connection becomes. That strong connection is what creates a deep, long-lasting relationship. The friendships and relationships that can emerge from self-disclosure are the rewards you get for taking the risk of sharing. Some people long for a deep relationship but are reluctant to engage the cost. Self-disclosure is just too risky. This is especially true if you have been hurt by another person. It takes time before you are willing to trust another person (if you ever decide to trust them again at all) and self-disclose information about yourself. In fact, risk and reward are such important factors in relationship decision-making that communication scholars have developed a theory of "social exchange" to explain it. This chapter will explore Social Exchange Theory and how it works, look at a parable Jesus told that illustrates Social Exchange Theory, and finally, explore some ways to make healthy exchange decisions in your own life.

Social Exchange Theory

The perceived exchange, or trade between the costs of a relationship and the rewards of being in that relationship, is the focus of Social Exchange Theory (SET).[2] Social Exchange Theory suggests that you seek out people who can give you rewards that are greater than or equal to the costs you encounter by being in that relationship. The reward can be any outcome you desire. A reward can be tangible, such as a paycheck or a car. It may also be intangible, such as power, friendship, or love. The costs of a relationship are outcomes that you are willing to exchange for the reward, such as a difficult working environment, lack of emotional support, emotional trauma, or unbalanced giving. When you encounter or participate in a relationship, you weigh the cost of being involved in that relationship. By weighing the costs versus the rewards, you can determine if a relationship is a good "deal."

To use an analogy, in graduate school, I had a job that was miserable. I worked by myself as a security guard, watching a company's parking lot full of delivery trucks on the graveyard shift (midnight to 8:00 am) to make sure no one broke into the lot and damaged or stole any of the trucks. Staying awake all night was a challenge, to say the least. But I made great money—over three times the minimum wage at that time. I chose to put up with the cost (lonely graveyard shift) because of the reward (a nice paycheck).

This process of "exchange" can be applied to more than just employment situations. You can apply the exchange principle to your human relationships. As a person of faith, you might determine that you would never date someone who did not share your faith. If a person who did not share your faith asks you on a date, you must decide how committed you are to rejecting that exchange (cost: dating a non-believer versus the reward: a potential romantic relationship). I have seen many people who desire a romantic relationship so much that they pay too high a "cost" to get into a relationship (dropping or compromising their standards). I have been blessed to have raised teenage daughters. None of them were allowed to date until they were age 16. When they were a few years away from age 16, I began asking them to come up with four to five of the most important qualities in a person they might be interested in dating (only one of the qualities could be physical; I wanted them to think about personality and character traits). The goal was to help them create a predetermined list of relationship "rewards" that they would not compromise so they would not just "settle" for someone who was attractive to them but did not have any of the predetermined qualities.

Social Exchange theorists argue that we consciously or unconsciously weigh relational alternatives. For instance, is one set of costs worth exchanging for another? When one of my daughters was a teenager, she discovered the harsh reality of these types of choices when she left one fast-food job for another fast-food job. The first job, to her, was horrible, and she was miserable doing such menial work (in her eyes) only to discover not long after she started the new job, that it was not much better than the first. Social exchange is about realizing that we have choices. We get to decide if the rewards received outweigh the costs of being in a relationship.

Sometimes it is necessary to compare multiple variables in the situation. You may have a person in your life that whenever your phone rings you sigh and struggle to decide whether you should answer the phone because you know you are going to spend the next two hours listening to them go on and on about something in their life. You have a long to-do list in front of you and you must decide if you are going to toss out the to-do list and answer the phone, or not answer because your to-do list involves things that must be done right now. On top of this, suppose that a piece of your decision-making criteria is that you feel the relationship with this person is very one-sided—they only reach out to you when they want something or need your time or attention. When you have tried to reach out to them, they are seldom available or have more important things to do. The person takes and takes from you (cost) yet you get very little in return (reward). You may determine that the cost to you of being in that relationship is too great compared to any rewards you might receive. These types of relationships may require us to either determine appropriate boundaries with the other person or maybe even terminate the relationship.[3]

These types of decisions can be scary when the risk is high. There are several questions we need to consider when making risky decisions. First, we must ask if we are judging our relationship against a realistic standard (I can find the perfect job or perfect mate). Second, we must ask if we have judged that person realistically (I have met someone who is perfect!). Third, we must ask ourselves what standards we are using for our rewards. It is very easy to fall into the fallacy of comparing our present relationship (job, mate) to other people's relationships and using them as a standard. You might argue, "Caleb and Mary always discuss every expenditure together before every purchase. Therefore, I want a relationship where the two of us discuss every expenditure too." The question that must be asked is, "Are Caleb and Mary a good or realistic standard to gauge a reward for *you*?" You and your partner are not Caleb and Mary. They have their own strengths and weaknesses that make that reward work for them. You and your partner do not have the same strengths and weaknesses. You have your own unique set of strengths and weaknesses. The right question to ask is, "What are the right rewards for *us*?"

It may sound like SET argues that we should not have role models, but that is not the case. Having role models is not wrong. In fact, role models can be very good in a variety of situations. I have turned to several people in my life whom I respect for ideas and suggestions when writing this book. However, when it comes to relationship decisions, looking through the theoretical lens of SET helps you to make sure that you do not make relational reward decisions based on wrong or unrealistic expectations or rewards. You also do not want to compromise and tolerate costs that are hurtful or harmful. Staying with a partner who abuses you (physically, emotionally, mentally) is never an acceptable "cost" for the reward of "at least I am in a relationship."

Mark 10:17–22 and The Rich Man and Heaven

While Social Exchange Theory is a helpful human tool, sometimes we need deeper spiritual insight to make wise relational decisions toward God and other people. Mark 10:17–22 is a wonderful biblical lens that provides insight into a man who had to evaluate his relationship with God:

> As Jesus started on his way, a man ran up to him and fell on his knees before him.
>
> "Good teacher," he asked, "what must I do to inherit eternal life?"

"Why do you call me good?" Jesus answered. "No one is good—except God alone.

You know the commandments: 'You shall not murder, you shall not commit adultery, you shall not steal, you shall not give false testimony, you shall not defraud, honor your father and mother.'"

"Teacher," he declared, "all these I have kept since I was a boy."

Jesus looked at him and loved him. "One thing you lack," he said. "Go, sell everything you have and give to the poor, and you will have treasure in heaven. Then come, follow me."

At this the man's face fell. He went away sad because he had great wealth.

This man wanted eternal life. For him, the reward of eternal life, or a relationship with God, was based on his perspective that the cost was merely obeying a set of commandments. That "exchange" seemed reasonable to him; he had kept all the commandments from his youth. Yet, ironically, despite his obedience, he seemed to be uncertain of his relationship and still felt the need to ask Jesus how to inherit eternal life. He appeared to be struggling with his relationship. The cost (keeping commandments) may have seemed too easy for such a great reward (eternal life and relationship with God).

Jesus pressed the man to consider one more cost, an even greater one—to sell everything he possessed and give the money to the poor. While merely keeping the commandments may have seemed like an easy cost, the man now had a cost that clearly seemed too much to bear. We are told in the passage that he grieved and went away. Perhaps he grieved because he was ashamed that he could not bear such a cost. Perhaps he grieved because he felt certain he had lost any chance at eternal life. We are not told why he grieved, but we are told that the man went away. This implied that he was willing to give up the reward of eternal life and a relationship with God because he could not bear the cost of selling his possessions.

This passage is generally not interpreted literally—that to have eternal life you must sell all your worldly possessions and "buy" your way into heaven. The passage is often interpreted as insight into what it means to give your life to God. God wants everything—your heart, your mind, your devotion, and your worship. This is the "exchange" that God requires of you—the reward of a life filled with God balanced against the cost of surrendering your life to him.

There is another level of exchange in our relationship with God that is tied to your calling to not just surrender your life to the Lord but also to engage in service and love toward other people. Jesus illustrated this level of exchange in Luke 14:12–14 (The Message):

> Then he turned to the host. "The next time you put on a dinner, don't just invite your friends and family and rich neighbors, the kind of people who will return the favor. Invite some people who never get invited out, the misfits from the wrong side of the tracks. You'll be—and experience—a blessing. They won't be able to return the favor, but the favor will be returned—oh, how it will be returned! —at the resurrection of God's people."

Jesus used this story to remind you that your relationship with God is reflected or expressed in your relationship with other human beings, especially the needy and oppressed. The passage shows that the rewards of investing in a relationship with other people may not come in the usual human form (i.e., they may not be able to repay us or even enhance our social network or status), but in loving them, you are loving Christ, who identified with the "least of these."[4] When you love, clothe, feed, care for other human beings, it is the same as doing it to Jesus. Mark 25:31–46 illustrates this promise:

> Then the King will say to those on his right, "Come, you who are blessed by my Father; take your inheritance, the kingdom prepared for you since the creation of the world. For I was hungry, and you gave me something to eat, I was thirsty and you gave me something to drink, I was a stranger and you invited me in, I needed clothes and you clothed me, I was sick, and you looked after me, I was in prison and you came to visit me."
>
> Then the righteous will answer him, "Lord, when did we see you hungry and feed you, or thirsty and give you something to drink? When did we see you a stranger and invite you in, or needing clothes and clothe you? When did we see you sick or in prison and go to visit you?" The King will reply, "Truly I tell you, whatever you did for one of the least of these brothers and sisters of mine, you did for me."

Unwrapping Social Exchange Theory

It is easy to get lost in relationships, whether just a friendship or a romantic relationship. Without determining clear boundaries for your life, you may never know that you are engaging in costs that are too much to bear. Sometimes you can even become complacent in the relationship. Over the years, I have often been amazed that a couple gets engaged when I know that one or both have shared with me some serious problems in the relationship. One young woman told me, "Yes, I know there are some problems, but I'd rather get married than be single again and have to start a whole new relationship with someone else." As you might guess that marriage did not last very long. The problems (costs) were not outweighed by the reward (being married). I have also had many individuals tell me, "Yes, we have some problems, but once we get married, it will be better, and it will all work out." Those marriages seldom last very long either. Those individuals find out that the potential reward (problems will change) seldom arrived, thus making the cost (a marriage with problems) too great to survive.

On the other hand, many people may decide to follow God (reward) but never fully grasp the cost of absolute surrender. Absolute surrender can be a difficult concept to understand. Everyone has different areas of their lives to surrender, and not everyone is going to struggle with the same costs. One person may be able to regularly tithe with great joy, while another person may covet their money so much they cannot even think of surrendering a tithe of any amount to the Lord. One person may be able to give their time to serve at their church, while another person may struggle to give their time to serve. One person may be able to let go and allow the Lord to heal them of the pain caused by someone who hurt them, while another person may refuse to surrender that pain and let it fester and eat away at their heart. The list can go on and on. What issue, hurt, pain, struggle, or commandment in your life are you unable to accept and entrust to God? Why is the cost too great that you are willing to sacrifice the reward of your relationship with God over it?

When it comes to your daily communication, what "possessions" does God ask you to let go of to be in a relationship with people? For me, I have several challenges I must consciously work on. When I am completely relaxed or just listening to someone, my family tells me I have a very grumpy look on my face. I am not grumpy, just totally relaxed. As a result, I must consciously put my facial nonverbals in check and make sure I am smiling when I am around people. I also do not like small talk (Hey, nice weather today. Think the Mariners can win it all this year?). It feels like unnecessary work and can drive me crazy. But making small talk (the cost) is a way to begin self-disclosing and connecting with other people (the reward). So, I have made myself learn to do it and try to enjoy it, because I never know when God is needing to use me in another person's life.

Another challenge is coming up with positive, affirming words for those I interact with because this takes work, and I may not naturally think of it in the middle of a conversation. I have made a vow to always try to say something positive to every person I talk to, complement them, comment on an article of clothing, or really listen to them (Chapter 8 in this book) so God can love that person through me. Do I always succeed? Good grief, no. I fail all the time. But sometimes I succeed, and God blesses and honors my efforts. A few years ago, I took a student to a conference to support her while she presented her research paper. The presentation was very nerve-wracking for her and when she finished, I knew she needed a boost of encouragement, even something simple. She did a really good job with her presentation. I prayed and asked the Lord, "Give me the right words to say." Not really thinking, I blurted out to her, "The student has surpassed the teacher!" She smiled and gave me a hug. I thought nothing of it, until recently when I watched a promotional video for our school and this student was interviewed on the video. Our school promises each student that they will "Be Known." My student told the story of giving her paper at a professional conference. She shared on the video that when I said that comment to her (that I had not thought through but just blurted out) it touched her core. I had no idea. I just knew that to love the Lord meant exchanging my comfort zone (not focusing on positive words with others) for my calling to follow God (love others with my words) and use my gift of communication to honor God.

Unwrapping the Costs and Rewards of Social Exchange

1. What, to you, is a reasonable cost to be in a relationship with someone—romantic or non-romantic?

2. Have you ever experienced a one-sided relationship—where the cost appeared or seemed much greater to you than for the other person? How did you feel in that relationship? Did it last or did it end? Why?

3. What expectations do you place on your friendships? What expecta-

tions do you place on your romantic relationships? How do you keep the two separate?

4. Do you sometimes expect more from other people than you give to them? Is there a friendship in your life that you feel you could give more to than you are currently giving? Explain your answer.

5. Do you ever expect more from God than you give to God? How do you resolve the inequity in that exchange?

Conclusion

All relationships involve a cost. We surrender time, money, energy, plans, and a whole host of tangible and intangible things to have jobs, boyfriends/girlfriends, spouses, families, and even vacations. The cost of a personal relationship with God is to surrender your life to him. That means you surrender your pride, your will, your money, your ego, and even your relationships to his will, but the reward of this exchange is almost beyond your grasp—a life guided and directed by the creator of the universe. If you approach your friendships and relationships with this same mentality, evaluating what you put into them versus what you expect out of them, you may see how selfish you are being. With some effort, however, you can balance the exchange in the friendship by using your gift of communication to honor God in that person and trust him for the reward. It may seem like a bit of a risk—like having to give up a sure thing of having $1000 to see what is behind door number one. But with God, we know for sure the curtain will never contain a giant panda bear Zonk! Now that is a deal I am willing to make.

• Prayer Prompt •

Father, what a blessing communication can be. Thank you for giving us your gift. Forgive me for the times that I have given too great of a cost to receive some sort of fleeting reward. Forgive me if I have been willing to exchange my faith, my values, or my life with you to win approval from another person or the world. Forgive me, too, when I have selfishly withheld loving communication from others because I did not see them as precious in your sight or worthy of my time. Give me wisdom to determine what costs and rewards are most important to me in my relationships. Help me find the balance between loving someone and letting them take and take from me to the point that the relationship is not healthy. In Jesus's name, Amen.

Chapter 9: Follow-Up Questions

1. Have you ever had to make a tough decision about a job, relationship, or situation where you had to weigh out the costs versus the rewards? How did you weigh the costs of that decision? What advice did you seek? What was the outcome of that decision?

2. When you first engaged in your relationship with God, what was your original perception of the cost to you versus the reward you were receiving? Has your perception of the original exchange changed or been modified? If it has changed, what has been the change?

3. Is there something in your life, like the rich man's possessions, that you know you need to let go of, but do not feel like you can? What makes losing it so great a cost that you are willing to give up the reward of a relationship with God in order to keep it?

4. What is the most important reward for you from a friendship? How hard or how easy has it been for you to find that reward in the people in your life? What has made it hard or easy?

5. What is the greatest cost you have paid for having another person in your life? Was it easy or hard for you to accept that cost? Why or why not?

Chapter 10

How Does That Make You Feel?

Communication Climate and Colossians 4:6

> I have come to the frightening conclusion that I am the decisive element. It is my personal approach that creates the climate. It is my daily mood that makes the weather. I possess tremendous power to make life miserable or joyous. I can be a tool of torture or an instrument of inspiration, I can humiliate or humor, hurt or heal. In all situations, it is my response that decides whether a crisis is escalated or de-escalated, and a person is humanized or de-humanized. If we treat people as they are, we make them worse. If we treat people as they ought to be, we help them become what they are capable of becoming.[1]
>
> —Haim G. Ginott

I HAVE BEEN BLESSED TO LEAD several student trips to various locations around the world as part of a program at my university called Juniors Abroad. Faculty take approximately 20 students each at the end of their junior year to different parts of the world for three weeks. One of my favorite countries to visit is Peru, and one of the biggest challenges I prepare my students for during the semester leading up to the trip is the different climates we will experience. We spend time in the capital, Lima, where it is pleasant but usually rains at the time of the year we travel. We then go to the Amazon River where the heat and humidity are stifling. After the Amazon, we head south to Cusco and Machu Picchu where we are above 10,000 feet and it is sunny and warm during the day but very cold at night. The final leg of the trip is a homestay on an island with Indigenous people on Lake Titicaca in southern Peru, which can take us to altitudes of 12,000-13,000 feet. The Indigenous homes have no heating, and the temperature is always freezing at night. The students are limited in the amount of luggage they can bring on the trip so packing clothing for everything from shorts and t-shirts for the Amazon to jackets and boots for the Andes Mountains can be challenging. It is unusual to experience such extreme climate changes in one trip, but it is the trip of a lifetime, so everyone figures out how to make it work.

Just like the Peru trip has different climates, so too, can our relationships experience different communication climates. Relationships can experience sunny and bright moments, rainy and dreary moments, hurricane and tornado moments, or cold and freezing moments. Whether the relationship is between work colleagues, family members, friends, or romantic partners, the climate can be determined by the type of language used by each person in the relationship. The quality of language used in relationships can be placed into two broad categories called confirming and disconfirming language. This chapter will define confirming and disconfirming language, examine how Scripture emphasizes the value of confirming language, and finally, explore ways to incorporate more confirming language in your daily communication.

Disconfirming versus Confirming Language

In the discipline of communication studies, disconfirming language refers to any language that conveys disregard or makes another person feel unvalued.[2] Disconfirming language can be subtle and passive, or blatant and mean. When speaking to someone, a person using disconfirming language would be more concerned about winning a conflict or criticizing the other person. Simple phrases can cut deep for the recipient. Telling a child "I can't believe you did that," or "You clearly were not thinking when you did that" can create a stormy or negative climate. Telling a work colleague "You clearly are not as experienced as you claimed to be" or "You do not seem interested in learning the culture of our company" can create a defensive, or dark and dreary, climate for the relationship. Calling a person a name or criticizing them will not only hurt them and cause them to become defensive, but it can cause a tornado if the person feels attacked or beaten down too much.

Chapter 7 highlighted the expectations we place on romantic partners with Expectancy Violations Theory (EVT). Disconfirming language is worse when used between people who claim to love each other. EVT explains why it is so hurtful when a romantic partner uses disconfirming language: we expect romantic partners to be kind and loving. Calling a romantic partner a negative name dehumanizes them and turns them into an object rather than a human being with value and worth. Any type of critical or sharp language will quickly turn a sunny relationship into a stormy relationship.

The opposite of disconfirming language is confirming language, which is any language that conveys value or makes another person feel valued.[3] Confirming language shows respect for the recipient as a human being who is loved and valued by God. It creates a positive, sunny, and warm climate for the relationship. A child can be reprimanded without negative language by asking "Help me understand why you made that choice." A work colleague can be asked, "Tell me what you think is the culture here at our company." Telling a romantic partner, "I am having a hard time understanding what you mean, tell me again" creates a more positive relational climate than saying, "As always, you make no sense and I have no idea what you are talking about."

Confirming language requires a conscious and intentional effort on the part of the sender. Disconfirming language comes easily due to our sinful nature. There is a part in all of us that wants to get the upper hand, to win an argument, to be defensive and attack someone who is critical of us. It often takes a conscious effort to stop, think, and intentionally use confirming language.

Over the years I have had to work hard on using confirming language. My personality is prone to reacting (and often overreacting) to situations and things people say rather than responding. I have a note on my office desk that I look at every day asking me "Are you responding or reacting?" Reacting usually involves disconfirming language—it is impulsive, unfiltered, and motivated by pride. The whole purpose of disconfirming language is to promote yourself while demoting the other person. Through the lens of these communication concepts, you can see that the language you choose directly impacts your relationships with other people. The lens of Scripture brings this reality into an even clearer focus.

Colossians 4:6 and Confirming Language

The Bible is filled with passages on selecting and managing our words with care. Colossians 4:6 commands the reader, "Let your conversation be always full of grace, seasoned with salt so that you may know how to answer everyone." Confirming language is speech filled with grace and love. Ephesians

4:29 implores the reader, "Let no corrupt communication proceed out of your mouth, but that which is good to the use of edifying, that it may minister grace unto the hearers."[4] When I read these types of verses, I want to say, "Aww, come on God, can't you give me just a little wiggle room?" Living a life of faith that honors God would be so much easier if I was commanded to "Let only a *little* corrupt communication" or "Let just *some* corrupt communication" proceed out of my mouth. I could do that. Yet, God instructs me to let "no" corrupt communication proceed out of my mouth. There is little room for interpretation here because "no" means, well… "no!"

God also provided a good synonym for disconfirming language with the words "corrupt communication." You are commanded in the Bible to love others.[5] When you love someone, you show respect for them as a human being created and loved by God. Disconfirming language corrupts our communication by turning it into a vehicle for disrespect and devaluation. Confirming language, words that make a person feel valued and loved, allows you to avoid corrupt communication.

Psalm 19:14 gives us deeper insight into the source and motivation for uplifting language. The Psalmist cried out to God and exclaimed, "May these words of my mouth and this meditation of my heart, be pleasing in your sight, O Lord, my rock, and my redeemer." The Psalmist gives insight into where confirming or disconfirming language comes from. From a faith perspective, you can see that it comes from your heart. The heart and the mouth are connected. One part of the body leads the other part of the body. You must start with a heart that wants to value the other person, to love them at all costs. This willing heart comes from you allowing God to control your heart. When the heart is right, then the mouth will follow.

Unwrapping Confirming Language

Learning to use confirming language can seem daunting. How do you always use words that make other people feel valued? It *sounds* hard. As I wrote above, I have struggled and wrestled with this calling my entire life (and probably will until I die). The day I was editing this chapter, my wife called me, and I was selfishly irritated that she called while I was writing, so I responded to her with a curt answer. As soon as I hung up, I returned to editing this chapter and was immediately convicted of my language use.

Everyone makes mistakes and sometimes fails to unwrap their gift in a way that honors God. That is OK. It is your heart that matters to God. Are you willing to honestly try to change your language style? If so, there are some tricks I have learned to try to improve the use of my gift. First, using confirming language does not mean you always have to agree with the other person. Remember Chapter 8 of this book and some of the listening skills addressed in that chapter? One of those skills was to avoid evaluative statements. Rather than tell a person how to feel ("Don't be mad") the chapter identified how to validate the emotion you hear ("You sound angry"). If I hear a particular emotion in a person's tone or words, I try to focus on that emotion. I will say, "You sound really frustrated by this," or "This is really bothering you, isn't it?" That does not mean that I agree that the topic justifies the emotion I am hearing. In fact, I sometimes can disagree 100% with the emotion. When someone complains to me about a spouse driving them crazy because they hang the toilet paper the wrong way, I know the problem is not about toilet paper. The problem is really something else. However, I can affirm what I hear, "The toilet paper thing really bothers you doesn't it?" By validating the emotions of the other person, that person feels valued and hopefully, loved.

Second, I have learned that if I disagree with a person on something, I do not have to resort to disconfirming language to "win" the argument. I have a colleague who is a master of this skill. They can disagree with someone on a topic that we are voting on as a faculty, but when they speak, they always start by pointing out one or two positive things about the proposal. This confirming language allows the opponent to feel valued. After they comment on a few positive things, they present some of the negative concerns but always phrase each point with "What I am uncomfortable with," or "What puzzles me here is . . .". They always soften the attack by acknowledging their emotions or feelings on the issue. I recently walked away from a heated faculty meeting and heard another colleague say to my colleague, "I am always amazed at how kindly you express your opposition to something." Using confirming language, even in conflict, is possible with work and effort.

Third, one way I have learned to measure my use of confirming language is to try to always ask myself, "How will my words make the other person *feel*?" True, we are not responsible for another person's emotions (covered in Chapter 5), but we are responsible for the words that come out of our mouths and how those words affect other people. Unfortunately, words can cut deeper, and hurt for longer, than you might imagine. I was speaking at a marriage retreat and a man came up to me at one of the breaks between sessions. He expressed his frustration with his marriage and how he struggled with his wife. Eventually, he told me that he had said to her, "If you died, I would not miss you." I wanted to scream at him and say "You are the biggest jerk I have ever met!" but instead, I simply asked him, "How do you think that made her feel?" He looked at me very puzzled and said, "What does that have to do with anything?" I suggested we meet after the seminar, and we could talk about this in greater detail. Unfortunately, he left and never came back to talk. He did not understand God's calling for us to use confirming language.

People in relationships are never going to agree on everything. Conflict is inevitable.[6] But if you stop and ask yourself, "How is what I am about to say going to make the other person feel?" and you cannot honestly say, "They will feel valued" then you need to stop and choose your words differently. Your human nature will beg you to toss out a mean zinger to "win" the argument, but that is your pride and your ego needing to "win" and God hates pride.[7] Instead, our words should be motivated by love—especially with those closest to us.

In romantic relationships, we expect confirming language from our partner. When you use disconfirming words, it stands out and hurts much more because the expectation of receiving confirming words was shattered. It is not enough to think, "I say lots of confirming things and only a few disconfirming things now and then. Why isn't that good enough?" Research has found that if couples have five times as many positive interactions as negative ones, they are likely to have happy and successful relationships.[8] That is a big ratio—five to one. That means every time you use a disconfirming word or statement, you will need to use five confirming statements just to break even. If you do the math, it can be overwhelming. If you say five or six disconfirming statements, you now need 25-30 positive statements just to break even, let alone try to get ahead. You have a choice of what type of language you use, so make it count.

A fourth way to practice using confirming language is to set a goal to always say something positive or complimentary to a person when you are talking to them. This can be as simple as "I like your shoes" or "I like your tie." Even if it is in a public setting like a meeting, you can always say, "I like the way my colleague is passionate about their position on this topic," or "I love the way you articulate your thoughts, you are very clear." Making a habit of saying positive things can become a part of your everyday life and that honors God.

I was attending a conference once and a friend of mine was overseeing a business meeting. Our allotted time for using the room we were in had expired, and another group was waiting outside to use the room for their meeting. Our group was hanging around and mingling and talking well past the time we should have exited. The employees of the conference center were getting impatient with our group and kept trying to get us to move out of the room, but it was not working. My friend who oversaw the meeting was also getting frustrated with our group, so he stepped to the microphone and instead of asking everyone to leave, he calmly and quietly said, "I love all the networking that is going on and I would love to invite you to continue our conversations outside in the hallway with me. So, everyone please follow me out into the hallway." It worked. Everyone made their way out of the room. I heard one of the group members say, "That is why I like working with Paul, he is such a kind man."

A fifth and final way to practice using confirming language is to try an exercise I give to my classes. I challenge my students to go one entire day without saying anything negative and write a brief paper about their experience. Usually not a single student makes it. I once had two students who were very sick with the flu and spent the day in bed sleeping. They made it, but only because they slept all day and did not speak to anyone. Being sick was what it took to win the challenge. Most students write about how hard it was and how they had to make a conscious effort to always stop and think before they spoke. Some students get frustrated and give up as early as breakfast and write about how impossible it was to say anything positive about the cafeteria food that morning. Some students work very hard at the challenge and make it through most of the day but eventually succumb to their human nature.

Your human nature finds it easy to use disconfirming language, but to be a "new person in Christ" means making every possible honest effort to use confirming language in your daily conversations.[9] Confirming language honors God by using his gift of communication in the way he intended it to be used. Disconfirming language misuses your gift.

5 Ways to Unwrap Confirming Language

1. Remember: Using confirming language does not mean that you must agree with the other person.

2. It is possible to disagree without using disconfirming language.

3. Before you speak ask yourself, "How will what I am about to say make the other person feel?"

4. Work on finding positive, confirming statements of some sort in every conversation you have. See if you can make it a habit in your daily life. Try to have five positive interactions for every negative interaction with another person.

5. Try to go an entire day without saying anything negative. See if you can make using confirming language a natural part of your everyday life.

Conclusion

Being in relationships can be like trying to pack for one of my student trips to Peru. In a relationship, no matter what type, you have the potential to experience every type of climate. Sometimes relationships are sunny and bright and everything is great. But sometimes the sun can get too hot, and the humidity kicks in like the Amazon Rainforest, and the relationship can be miserable. Other times, the challenges and struggles of life can cause a relationship to be rainy and dreary and you must use language that will provide umbrellas to protect you from the misery you feel. Whatever the climate of a relationship, your language choices directly affect the climate.

The Bible is clear about what type of language you are to use. Your sinful, human side is drawn to disconfirming language, the use of words that dehumanize another person and make them feel less valued while also helping you feel like you win conflicts and are the better person (which feeds your pride and ego). Instead, God calls you to use confirming language, language that makes another person feel valued, or loved in the way God commands you to love one another.

• Prayer Prompt •

Father, thank you for your gift of communication. Thank you for giving me so much ability to control how I use your gift. Forgive me when I have reacted too quickly to a message and caused someone to feel less valued. Forgive me for letting my pride take control of my tongue and using disconfirming language just so I could win a conflict. Help me to respond to messages by stopping and filtering my words before I speak. Please help me remember to ask myself "How is what I am about to say going to make the other person feel?" and then give me the courage to close my mouth, think again, and choose confirming language. In Jesus's name, Amen.

Chapter 10: Follow-Up Questions

1. Is it easy for you to use disconfirming language? If yes, what makes it so easy?

2. Is it hard for you to use confirming language all the time? Why or why not?

3. Try to go an entire day without saying anything negative. How did that work for you? Did you make it?

4. How many of the five ways of engaging confirming language seem realistic to you? Why? What are some things you can do to try to engage in confirming language in your everyday communication?

5. Do any of the five ways of engaging confirming language seem unrealistic to you? Why? What is keeping you from engaging those steps in your everyday communication?

Chapter 11

The Root of All Evil

Conflict and Proverbs 6:16–19

So, the first thing that happens in a conflict is that we choose a side, because that's easier than trying to hold two thoughts in our heads at the same time. The second thing that happens is that we seek out facts that confirm what we want to believe—comforting facts, ones that permit life to go on as normal. The third is that we dehumanize our enemy.[1]

—Fredrik Backman

When you say something really unkind, when you do something in retaliation your anger increases. You make the other person suffer, and he will try hard to say or to do something back to get relief from his suffering. That is how conflict escalates.[2]

—Thich Nhat Hanh

SEVERAL YEARS AGO, I SERVED as a member of the board of directors of an organization. This organization hired several outside contractors for various work projects. One contractor received a great deal of work and billed us annually for hundreds of thousands of dollars. Unfortunately, one day the contractor had a run-in with a member of the organization and said some inappropriate things to the organizational member. A complaint was filed and brought to the board. I spoke to the organizational member before the meeting and discovered that all they were looking for was an apology from the contractor.

The contractor came to the board meeting and presented their defense. The Board listened and then said, "I am sure you regret this unfortunate situation and are sorry for what was said by everyone." I was clearly trying to lead them to, at the very least, admit that they regretted the situation. If the contractor would just say that much, the organizational member would accept it as an apology, and we could all move on. Unfortunately, the contractor locked down and said they had no regrets. The Board then explained to them that if there were no regrets and the organizational member did not withdraw their complaint, then based on the by-laws of the organization, we would have to terminate our relationship with the contractor (costing the vendor hundreds of thousands of dollars in revenue). I tried again and again to get the contractor to just admit they regretted the verbal exchange but had no success. After an hour or two of discussion, the Board was left with no choice but to terminate our business with the contractor.

This conflict event reminded me of two different perspectives people can take when approaching a conflict. This chapter will look at those two different approaches, explore the fallout from selecting each option, and then see what the Bible teaches about conflict, before looking at some practical ways to approach conflict without damaging relationships.

Toxic Conflict

When approaching a conflict, you have a choice about how you can approach it. Some people, like the vendor in my opening story, approach with the mindset, "How can I win this conflict?" This approach means that everything the person thinks, says, or does nonverbally is all focused on just one thing—winning. The person is usually defensive, locked down, uses disconfirming language, and is willing to sacrifice the relationship to win the conflict. The contractor was willing to lose the contract with our organization and lose a great deal of money to win the conflict.[3] The contractor did not even have to apologize, they just had to express regret (which I tried to get them to do), but they would not.

A second approach to conflict is to engage in with the mindset, "How can we resolve this conflict?" This approach means that everything the person thinks, says, or does nonverbally is focused on just one thing—resolution. Just from the two words used (win versus resolve) it is easy to see the difference between the approaches. Using a resolution approach rarely involves pride, ego, locking down, stubbornness, or any of the other defensive postures a person can take. Resolution means accepting the fact that miscommunication happens and that is OK.[4] Resolution seeking also means focusing on confirming language—words that communicate value and worth—rather than disconfirming language—words that communicate devaluation.[5] Resolving a conflict also represents a commitment to preserving the relationship with the other person.

When one or more people enter a conflict with the mindset of winning, the conflict can easily spiral downward, become destructive, and create a toxic environment resulting in a toxic relationship. Psychologist John Gottman studied couples for decades and found four different communication patterns that guaranteed which couples were more likely to divorce.[6] The first communication pattern that is destructive to couples is criticism, where partners attack each other's character. Rather than express frustration with another person using "I" language, (Chapter 5)—"I wish you had not been late, we are going to miss the concert"—a critical response attacks the person's character and connects the event in question to the person as a whole—"You are so selfish, you never think of anyone but yourself." Once a person's character is attacked, they will naturally become defensive to protect themselves. Critical attacks on the person's character communicate that you find fault in who they are as a person. This criticism leads to problems in the relationship, especially in a romantic relationship where a person says, "I love you," yet uses critical comments. In romantic relationships, you want the other person to think you are flawless, wonderful, and loving. You want to feel unconditional love and acceptance from your romantic partners. Criticism does not convey that message. Criticism destroys trust and slowly erodes the foundation of a relationship.

A second sign of a toxic relationship is the presence of defensiveness. When a person feels threatened, usually by a critical or attacking comment, that person will put up a wall, fight to preserve themselves, and return the attack. When one person tells another, "You are never on time," the recipient does not appreciate the lack of recognition for times when they have been on time and responds defensively saying, "You are worse than I am!" Both partners in the relationship begin to spiral downward and the conflict approach does very little to resolve the problem. Instead, this approach does a great deal to make the relationship more toxic.

The third sign of a toxic relationship is when one or both partners in a relationship express contempt for the other person. Contempt is evident when partners speak to each other with words that belittle or demean the other person. Contempt is evident if either person engages in verbal jabs such as name-calling ("You are so stupid!") or sarcastic barbs ("Oh, *that* was kind").[7] Contempt is also communicated through nonverbal communication. Eye rolls and audible sighs or breaths, often mixed with words, are an indicator of contempt. Rolling your eyes while saying, "Oh that was brilliant," conveys contempt for that person. The words are designed to demean or belittle, not uplift or value the person.[8] In fact, when a nonverbal act of contempt is combined with a verbal statement of contempt, it is nearly impossible to receive a message other than one of contempt.

The fourth, and final sign of toxic conflict is stonewalling. This occurs when one or both partners in a relationship shuts down conversation either verbally ("I'm not going to talk about this") or nonverbally (One person walking out of the room while the other person is speaking). Stonewalling is very dangerous because it represents an ultimate act of power—the person who stonewalls is taking control of the conversation. "I" am shutting this down, "I" am not going to talk about it, "I" am going to walk out of the room or hang up the phone so you cannot talk to me. Such acts of power show very little respect for the other person. When a power standoff happens in a relationship through stonewalling, it is very hard for each person in the relationship to feel value or worth.

Here is a brief example illustrating a toxic conflict resolution conversation containing all four elements, taken from a popular interpersonal communication textbook:

- Partner 1: "You overdrew our account again; can't you do anything right?" (**Criticism**)

- Partner 2: "Hey, don't blame me, you're the one who spends most of the money." (**Defensiveness**)

- Partner 1: "At least I have better math skills than a first grader. Way to go, Einstein." (**Contempt**)

- Partner 2: "Whatever" (said while walking out of the room). (**Stonewalling**)[9]

From a theoretical perspective, it is easy to see how this type of communication is not constructive for building trust and transparency in any relationship, let alone a marriage. Any one of these four components of toxic communication can feed off each other and create toxic conflict that fails to resolve anything. Approaching conflict with a "How can I win?" mentality is almost guaranteed to lead to some form of toxic conflict communication patterns.

Proverbs 6:16–19 and Toxic Conflict

The need to "win" a conflict is usually driven by pride. "I" will win this conflict, "I" will stonewall and shut down dialogue, "I" will crush you with criticism or contempt. Each one of these statements is driven by pride, a need to be in control and feel you have power. Proverbs 6:16–19 (NKJV) communicates very clearly how God feels about pride:

> These six things the LORD hates, Yes, seven are an abomination to Him: A proud look, A lying tongue, Hands that shed innocent blood, A heart that devises wicked plans, Feet that are swift in running to evil, A false witness who speaks lies, And one who sows discord among brethren.

The very first item on the list of things God hates is pride. Pride drives our need for power and power drives our need to use any, or all, of the four postures of toxic conflict.

Much of Scripture requires us to set aside our pride and our drive for power. Ephesians 4:29 declares that you are to "Let no corrupt communication proceed out of your mouth, but that which is good to the use of edifying, that it may minister grace unto the hearers." As I wrote earlier in this book, this verse leaves no wiggle room for negotiation. "No corrupt communication" means "*No* corrupt communication." All four of the identifiers of toxic communication in relationships are forms of corrupt communication. From a faith lens, you can see that God commands us to have none of it. It is pride that drives you to want to hurt another person, even someone you love. God commands in Ephesians 5:25 for husbands to "Love your wives even as Christ also loved the church." Christ never treated the church (people of faith) with criticism, defensiveness, contempt, or stonewalling. Therefore, to love your spouse in the same way, your conflict management with him or her must not contain any corrupt communication—criticism, defensiveness, contempt, or stonewalling.

Avoiding Toxic Conflict Strategies

What is your usual approach to a conflict? Do you see a conflict as something to be "won"? If so, that is the first place to begin to develop healthy conflict communication skills. The desire to "win" is natural and part of being human. You were raised from a young age to "win" everything from athletic activities and music competitions and to "win" by getting good grades, getting a good job, getting promoted, and even raising a good family. Culturally, you are driven to push and push to be the best at whatever you attempt.

It becomes hard to separate your drive to win from your pride. I have never heard of any athletic team that begins their season saying, "Our goal this year is to be the worst team in the league. We want to be the worst at everything we do." An athlete's pride motivates them to be the best they can be, to excel, and to win. As a result, when you enter a conflict management situation, wanting or needing to win is almost second nature. It becomes a part of who you are. That's why separating your pride from your conflict communication strategies takes a concerted effort. You must be intentional in your word choice and approach to conflict. You can begin to change your conflict strategies by committing to approach every conflict situation with the goal of "How can we *resolve* this conflict." Committing to this mentality can change even how you approach a conflict conversation. The defensive walls can come down. Hurt and anger can avoid being projected. Valuing the other person as a human being worthy of respect can flow from your words.

Simply telling a person to avoid negative conflict management communication is easy, but changing your communication patterns can be challenging. First, when you approach a conflict situation and you feel driven or motivated to win the conflict, be honest and ask yourself, "Why?" What is so important about this situation that you let your pride consume the conversation and corrupt communication flow from your mouth like a river? Remember Proverbs 6:16–19. God hates pride. Your pride can cause you to need to win a conflict, leading you to be critical, defensive, show contempt, or stonewall. These communication behaviors clearly do not honor God and should be avoided.

Next, commit to avoiding criticism. This means never saying anything negative about the other person's character or personality. Focus on using "I" language. Rather than saying "You are always late" try to use phrases like "I do not understand why it is so challenging to get here on time" or "Can you please help me understand why it is challenging for you to get here on time?" Remember, any time you attack the other person, especially if you attack who they are as a person, you invite defensiveness from the person you attack. Their walls will go up and they will usually respond with similar attacks. The conflict can quickly get diverted onto a completely different topic and the original topic is lost in the mess.

Remember the role that defensiveness can play in a conversation. Certain comments can always create defensiveness in a person. When you know those statements and choose to use them to attack the person and make them defensive, this is the behavior of a person trying to win the conflict and letting their pride drive the conversation. You are clearly choosing corrupt communication as your conflict management tool and not using your gift of communication in a way that honors God.

Watch out for the use of contempt in your words. If you are close to the other person (i.e., a romantic relationship) then you know their fears and struggles. If you make any reference to those fears or struggles in a way that belittles or demeans that person, then you are choosing contempt. To choose contempt as your conflict strategy means you are letting your pride control your choices. You are knowingly trying to belittle or demean the other person and you do not care. Again, that is pride.

Finally, recognize and avoid stonewalling at all costs. Never hang up the phone on someone mid-sentence to intentionally stop the conversation. Never walk out of the room while the other person is talking. Never interrupt and talk over the other person so loudly that they cannot be heard. Anything that cuts off the conflict conversation intentionally is called stonewalling. That is an abuse of power because you are determining that this conversation will end now. In a relationship where partners are equal, neither person should try to exercise that type of power.[10]

Remember Chapter 10 in this book on the use of confirming and disconfirming language? When you enter any conflict conversation, try to use confirming language, language that makes the other person feel valued. Your word choice can de-escalate a situation. The moment you say something that causes the other person to feel devalued that is going to escalate the situation. You may think by escalating the situation you win the conflict, but all it does is dishonor God, by spewing corrupt communication from your mouth, which poisons the relationship making it likely that the other person will want to use similar communication to get back at you in the future.

5 Ways to Unwrap Your Conflict Conversations

1. Commit to entering all conflict conversations with the mentality of "How can we resolve this conflict?"

2. Remove criticism from your conflict options. Commit to never attack a person's character or personality in a conflict.

3. Commit to avoid creating a defensive climate when you engage in a conflict. Use "I" words to explain your feelings and your thoughts on the situation. Remember, as soon as you attack the other person in any way, they can become defensive and escalate the conflict tension.

4. Believe that contempt is never an option. Commit to never belittling or demeaning the other person. This includes both verbal and nonverbal communication.

5. Never stonewall. Commit to never hanging up the phone, walking out of the room, or flexing your power in any way to cut off the conversation and exert control over the situation. Remember that stonewalling is an act of power, driven by pride.

Conclusion

To this day, I still wonder why the contractor for the organization I worked with in my opening story was willing to give up so much money just to win the conflict with the member of the organization. Hundreds of thousands of dollars were at stake. Unfortunately, they are not alone. Many people, daily, choose to win a conflict no matter what the cost—money, friends, family, or even spouses. You learn as a child how to flex your power on the playground ("We play by my rules, or I am taking my ball and going home") and unfortunately, those patterns can follow you into adulthood. To change this learned, childish behavior, you have to consciously choose not to let power drive your adult conversations.

It is difficult to navigate conflict without the emotion of anger rearing its ugly head. The following chapter is devoted to exploring the emotion of anger and providing some constructive ways to navigate that emotion.

This chapter has barely scratched the surface of conflict management, but hopefully, it has helped you see areas for needed improvement in your conflict management communication. Working from these concepts, my prayer is that you will understand you have choices and options when it comes to conflict management conversations. You can choose to honor God, or you can choose to not honor God based on your own personal convictions. The ball is truly in your court.

• Prayer Prompt •

Father, thank you for your gift of communication. Thank you for the power to choose the words we use to communicate. Forgive me when my pride drives me to try to win a conflict. Forgive me for thinking I need power in a conflict, and using toxic conflict strategies. I pray for wisdom to know how to use words that will honor you and not corrupt my relationships. I pray for the strength to stop and think before I speak so that I can love others with my words, even when we disagree. I pray this in Jesus's name, Amen.

Chapter 11: Follow-Up Questions

1. What does it mean to you to approach a conflict with a mindset of "How can we resolve this conflict?" What are some ways you can try to do that?

2. Can you think of a time in a conflict conversation when someone treated you with criticism, defensiveness, contempt, or stonewalling? What form of toxic conflict was it and what did that person do/say? How did it make you feel and how did you respond?

3. Can you think of a time in a conflict conversation that you used one or more of the toxic conflict strategies (criticism, defensiveness, contempt, or stonewalling)? What drove you to use that option? How did your chosen strategy affect the overall conflict situation? How did it turn out?

4. Do you agree or disagree that toxic conflict strategies are driven by our pride? Why or why not?

5. Is it possible to let "No corrupt communication proceed out of your mouth"? (Ephesians 4:29). How realistic is that goal and what can you do to try to achieve it?

Chapter 12

Knowing When to Walk Away

Communicating Anger and Ephesians 4:26

The longer I live, the more I observe that carrying around anger is the most debilitating to the person who bears it.[1]

—Katharine Graham

Speak when you are angry, and you will make the best speech you will ever regret.[2]

—Ambrose Bierce

I LIKE TO MAKE A BOLD STATEMENT in class that usually gets a rise out of many of the students. When studying conflict, I declare, "God has made us to be conflictual beings." Some students shrug their shoulders and say "Whatever." A few students have the look in their eyes that they "get it." But many students usually say, "What are you talking about? God did not do that." These students remind me that the Bible is filled with verses on love and commands for us to love others. For many people of faith, the goal is to get along and love others, to always look for a peaceful connection with others, and to not have conflict. I then ask the class, "Do you believe that God made you a 'special, one of a kind, unique, no one else like you' individual?" The students agree and say, "Yes." I then ask them, "Do you believe God gives you free will to say and do what you want, regardless of whether it is right or wrong?" Again, the students reply, "Yes." I explain, "Then, no matter how well you get along with another person, at some point, you are going to disagree. You and I cannot be unique, one of a kind, and always agree on everything."

Disagreements with other people are inevitable and those disagreements can create conflict. The presence of conflict is generally not what creates relational problems. Problems arise when you manage, or more likely,

121

mismanage the conflict. When someone disagrees with you about something and attacks your beliefs, your natural reaction is to become defensive. If you feel you are being treated unfairly you may fight for equality. If you believe there is a better way to do something, you may try to convince others to follow your idea. If you believe strongly in a particular religious or political ideal, you may feel compelled to try to share your ideas with the goal of the other person agreeing with your position.

Regardless of the reason, your differences in ideas and beliefs place you in a state of conflict with another person. Tension often emerges in a conflict and emotions can get in the way. Perhaps the strongest emotion to navigate in a conflict is anger, especially if the conflict involved any type of attack on your character, your beliefs, or your self-image. This chapter will explore anger and the triggers that can set anger in motion, see what the Bible teaches regarding anger, and finally explore some simple steps you can take to better manage anger when it is present.

Exploring Anger

In small doses, anger is an appropriate, normal, and healthy emotion. Everyone experiences anger. Without anger, you might never try to stand up for yourself when you have felt wronged or protect your needs (emotional, psychological, or physical). But when anger is misunderstood or mismanaged, it can easily and quickly become a deterrent to healthy communication. When your anger negatively affects others, keeps you from performing your job or other tasks, affects your health, or is too intense for both you and those around you, then your anger has been mismanaged and is a problematic emotion.

To begin exploring anger, you need to understand that many researchers have identified some sort of trigger as the starting place of anger.[3] Anger triggers can be people, places, situations, and things that set off negative feelings. Usually, anger is an expression of a deeper, repressed emotion or feeling. If you are cut off in traffic by someone, you might get angry and yell at the driver, not because you are hypersensitive about others' driving, but because you had experienced some sort of event at work or school, that made you feel hurt, sad, or wronged. You were not able to express that feeling to the person that you felt treated you wrongly (like your boss) so you just buried the emotion and let it simmer. Your yelling at the other driver is not so much about them cutting into your lane. You are yelling to release the repressed emotions that you have been repressing all day. The other car becomes your trigger.

There are many different types of anger triggers for everyone. One unique anger trigger I want to highlight in this chapter is fear. Research has found a connection between anger and fear.[4] If you are like me, when I first heard that connection, I thought, "What in the world does fear have to do with my anger?" The answer to that question is found in exploring how the expression of anger can become a learned pattern triggered by fear.

As a child, you experience all sorts of threats and fears. If an infant feels hungry or is in discomfort, they fear going hungry or being in discomfort, so they cry to get fed or changed because they do not have words yet to express their needs. If a toddler has a toy taken away from them, they fear never seeing the toy again, so they get angry and throw a tantrum. A first grader is afraid of other kids laughing at them for a mistake in class, so they get angry and start throwing things around in the room. In each scenario, the behavior is reinforced and becomes a pattern—some sort of fear triggered a reaction of anger. The infant learned that when they felt hungry and cried they got fed. When a toddler throws a tantrum over a lost toy, they usually get attention in some form and learn to behave that way over and over.

As a child matures into adolescence and then adulthood, the pattern can become embedded in their communication style if they are not taught how to redirect their feelings, use words, or express their anger in a positive way. When a grown adult feels fear because their significant other said or did something that they perceived as a threat, it is easy to resort to the anger pattern because it was reinforced as a child. An emotionally mature adult may have been taught how to control their anger as well as recognize and address the fear. However, if an adult was never taught how to use their words and identify emotions in a healthy way, then their childhood anger patterns may take over. If you have ever had a conversation with an adult but felt like you were talking with a child, chances are, emotionally you were. There is a good chance that the person struggled with emotional maturity and lacked the tools needed to communicate emotions as an adult. Remember, all communication tools are taught. If a child was never taught how to manage their negative emotions in a healthy way, then they will resort to the only communication style they know—anger.

The way to address the anger trigger is to back up the pattern and ask, "What fear am I experiencing that is triggering my anger?" If you find yourself getting angry at your boss, what fear is driving your anger? Are you afraid of a poor performance review? Do you fear getting fired? Is your boss treating you unfairly or is there inequity in how the boss treats men and women? These are all valid fears that can justify your feelings of anger. However, rather than express your anger by being insubordinate and yelling at your boss, you need to back up the anger pattern and address the fear. Perhaps your boss asked you to stay late but you really need to get home and watch your children play a soccer game. You feel angry at your boss and use disconfirming language by complaining about how unfair it is to be asked to stay late. Instead, you could back up the anger cycle and ask yourself, "What am I afraid of?" and realize you are afraid that if you say no, then you will get fired. You can then reason that you have been with the company for over ten years, and have stellar performance reviews, so your job is secure. Therefore, being afraid you will be fired is somewhat irrational and not a valid fear. From a theoretical lens, you can see that by identifying the triggers of your anger, you can avoid the negative pattern of mismanaged anger.

It is important to note that not all fear leads to anger. You can fear a tornado but not be angry at it. However, if the tornado destroyed your home and you now fear that you will be homeless, you might express anger at God for allowing the tornado. Or you could be angry at the local tornado watch organization for not sending a faster warning signal if you lost a loved one in the tornado.

Ephesians 4:26 and Communicating Anger

God was very clear in the Bible and instructed us to never, ever be angry, right? Wrong. God experiences anger. All you need to do is read through the Old Testament and you will see God being angry at some individual or group quite often.[5] Jesus expressed anger on various occasions.[6] Since you are made in the image of God, and God experiences anger, then you are going to experience anger. It is what you do with the anger and how you communicate it that is important to God.

Ephesians 4:26 provides very clear guidelines on how to navigate anger: "In your anger, do not sin. Do not let the sun go down while you are still angry." God acknowledged that he gave you the emotion of anger, but you are not to sin when you express that anger. God draws a line that you are not to cross. From a faith perspective, you can see that when you cross that line, it becomes sin. But how do you know when you have crossed that line? Chapter 10 explored the role of confirming versus disconfirming language. Any time you use disconfirming language to express your anger, that would be a clear sign that you may have crossed the line. If I feel anger toward my wife and call her "stupid" or some other name, I have clearly sinned in the expression of my anger. This raises the question "How do I use confirming language to express my anger?" Am I supposed to say, "I am so happy I am angry?" No, of course not. But you have a choice. I have raised five children, and they have often made choices that caused me to feel anger. Sometimes I became so angry at their poor choices that I had to say, "I cannot talk to you about it right now. You are in trouble, but I do not want to talk to you in anger. I will talk to you later, but right now, just go to your room."

Unwrapping the Gift of Godly Communication When You Feel Anger

Fear is a large part of many people's lives. I have seen very strong people of faith crippled by some sort of fear—whether it is fear of rejection, fear of lack of acceptance, fear of conflict, fear of loneliness, fear of hurt, or fear of failure. Everyone has at least one fear that can cripple them and bring their life to a crashing halt. When I was in college, I competed on my school's speech and debate team. I was so afraid of failing, that when I did not make it into the final round and win, I got angry and would not talk to anyone. I pushed people away. Eventually, my teammates started avoiding me. My behavior was embarrassing and when I look back on it now, I am ashamed of my behavior and regret the relationships I hurt. Years later when I was in graduate school and studying this topic, I realized the fear behind my behavior, and I got help to address my fear of failure.

When you start to experience anger building inside of you, it is helpful to ask yourself, "What fear or threat is driving my anger?" If you can identify the fear or threat driving the anger, then you can address it. When one of my children leaves the house without a jacket on a cold, winter morning, I tell them to put on a jacket. If my child pushes back and says they are fine, I might get angry and tell them to put on a jacket, now. What is behind my anger? I am afraid my child will get sick from the cold and then I will have to take time off work to take care of them. My anger is partly driven by my selfishness. I do not want the inconvenience of having to take care of a sick child. Once I understand the threat driving my anger, I can address the threat. Will my child really get sick? Will I really be inconvenienced? Maybe, maybe not. But identifying and addressing the threat can help me to let go of the anger.

Sometimes anger is justified. You may experience an act of injustice and be treated with prejudice. You may get passed over for a promotion or a raise you felt you deserved. You fear being insignificant or walked upon. Identifying the fear or the threat may not make the anger go away, but it identifies for you the core issue behind the anger. You can then address the issue without the need to lash out and act upon your anger.

You are created with emotions, including fear which can lead to anger. You are accountable to God for what you do with your fears and your anger. Perhaps the biggest revelation you can have about fear comes from 2 Timothy 1:7, "For God has not given us the spirit of fear; but [a spirit] of power, and of love, and of a sound mind." When you experience fear, you must realize that it is not from God. God does not have any fear to give you. There is no fear in heaven. What kind of trigger is fear in your life? Do you struggle with the expression of anger that hurts you, those around you, or even your school or work performance? It may be necessary for you to get some help to figure out how to navigate the fear trigger.

One way to be angry, but not sin, is to avoid name-calling. Name-calling is one of the strongest forms of disconfirming language. When I am expressing my anger towards someone and I use their name, "Mike, I am very uncomfortable with what you said," I acknowledge Mike by his first name, and that humanizes him. It helps him feel valued which is confirming language. But when I choose to call him a name— "You are such a jerk, you just don't listen or care," I dehumanize Mike.[7] He is no longer a person, "Mike," he is an object, a jerk. Mike will clearly not feel valued by my language and that means I am using disconfirming language.

Another idea to keep in mind for navigating anger is to ask yourself, "Why is it so important for me to hurt the other person right now with what I say?" What threat or fear is driving your need to express your anger with mean, hurtful, or disconfirming words? Ask yourself, "Is what I am about to say, really so important, that I need to belittle or dehumanize the other person?" Remember Chapter 6 and the role language can play in trying to maintain position, power, or status. Ask yourself, "What threatened me so much that I feel the need to use language that will move me up the hierarchical ladder and move the other person down the ladder?"

Finally, remember that relationships are built on trust. You only self-disclose to someone when you trust them. For a relationship to move forward, the people in that relationship must self-disclose. Several studies have demonstrated that increased self-disclosure can improve troubled marriages.[8] Therefore, it is essential in all relationships to build trust, so there is self-disclosure, and the relationship can move forward and grow. In his book *The Seven Habits of Highly Effective People*, author Stephen Covey used the metaphor of an "emotional bank account" to describe "the amount of trust that's been built up in a relationship."[9] In relationships, especially romantic ones, I call this a trust account. Every time you speak to someone in a relationship, you either make a deposit or a withdrawal from your relational trust account. The number of deposits you place in your trust account becomes important when you say or do something that makes a withdrawal from the account. If you have only deposited a small amount in the account, when you lash out in anger and use disconfirming language, you make a giant withdrawal from that account.

Using this trust account metaphor, it is helpful if you stop and ask yourself, "Is what I am about to say going to make a deposit or a withdrawal from my trust account with this person?" If the answer is, "A withdrawal" or "I don't know," then another step is needed before you speak. Try to find one positive thing to say before you say your negative statement. Remember the five-to- one ratio of positive to negative comments noted previously in Chapter 10? While five positive statements may not be realistic when you are angry, try to find one point of agreement with the other person and say that positive statement before your negative statement. This could be something simple like, "I agree with you that what I did was not thoughtful, and I regret that, but I also want to add that I was uncomfortable with what you said to me."

Another option I try is to make myself say a quick prayer. It is hard to lash out in anger at a person when you are praying for them in your heart. Even if the prayer is a simple plea, "God, help me, I do not know what to do or say," a prayer can create the pause you need before you speak. If it is possible, I try to tell the other person what is going on. I have often told my children, "I am really angry right now and I do not want to speak to you in anger, so I need a few minutes to collect myself." This makes me very vulnerable to my children, but it shows my transparency and my commitment to love them as the Lord has commanded me. Find what works for you to allow you to be transparent and honest about your emotions but also allows you to address the situation productively and honor God. Walking away or slamming the door neither addresses the situation nor honors God.

Another anger pattern that can destroy relationships is when a person uses anger to manipulate another person. I often hear statements such as, "Oh, I do not want to go shopping with Mary, but if I say 'no' she will get mad." Mary has used anger to manipulate people to get them to do what she wants. She has not learned the importance of naming and owning her own emotions (Chapter 5) and building trust based on authentic transparency and honesty. Many people fear anger especially if they grew up in a home where anger was used to control the home ("Don't get Dad mad or else"). Mary has obviously expressed her anger in such a way that her friends fear her anger. This fear allows Mary to control the relationship and get her way. Obviously, this is not what God meant by "Be angry and sin not." Manipulation and control are driven by pride and this book has noted how God feels about pride on more than one topic. A person who uses anger to control relationships really needs to seek help to resolve the fears behind the anger.

5 Ways to Unwrap Godly Anger Management

1. When you feel angry, ask yourself: what is the fear behind my anger or what threat do I feel?

2. Stop name-calling. It is dehumanizing and will only provoke reciprocated anger.

3. Ask yourself, "Why do I need to hurt the person I am talking to with angry words?"

4. Ask yourself, "Is what I am about to say going to make a deposit or a withdrawal to my relational trust account?" Remember the "five positive comments for every one negative comment" in Chapter 10. If the answer is "a withdrawal," then ask yourself if you have made enough deposits in your relational account.

5. When you feel angry and your anger is justified, make sure you do not let the anger speak for you. Take a break, walk away, count to 10 or 20, or whatever number you need to make sure you speak in love.

Conclusion

Many years ago, country singer Kenny Rogers recorded a song called "The Gambler" about a man who had mastered the art of gambling. In the chorus of the song, the gambler shared insight on how to be a winning gambler. Rogers sang, "You have to know when to hold 'em, know when to fold 'em, know when to walk away, know when to run." In many ways, communicating anger in a relationship is very similar. A gambler's decision on what to do with their cards is like you knowing what to do with your anger. Does anger control what you say, or do you control how you communicate your anger? Do you know when to say nothing? I would not recommend that you "turn and walk away" like stonewalling (Chapter 11), but it does demonstrate self-control when you know to stop talking and just listen.

Conflict in a relationship is inevitable. God created us as unique individuals who should respect and care for one another, but sin has poisoned our relationships with selfishness, hurtfulness, and mistrust. God knew that fear and anger would be a part of your relationships as a result, so he inspired the words of Ephesians 4:26 to guide you in how you express your anger. You sin when you let fear control you, or when you call the other person names, or when your words make withdrawals from your relational trust accounts. These are just a few ways that anger can lead to sin. When we understand how to feel and navigate the emotion of anger, and we exercise self-control to not sin, we are on the right path to healthy communication.

• Prayer Prompt •

Father, thank you for your gift of communication. Thank you for giving me so much ability to control how I use your gift. Forgive me when I have let anger control my communication and I have sinned. Forgive me for my pride that feels the need to hurt or dehumanize another person. I pray for wisdom and insight to know when to not say anything or turn and walk away. I also ask for wisdom to know how to communicate my anger in love using words that build trust and honor you. In Jesus's name, Amen.

Chapter 12: Follow-Up Questions

1. How do you generally express your anger? Do you feel that you can control your anger or does your anger control you?

2. Think of a recent situation in which you felt angry. What triggered your anger? Was it fear? If so, was the fear justified? Why or why not?

3. Is name-calling a problem for you? Do you understand what it means to dehumanize a person? What are three things you can do to stop using name-calling as an anger strategy?

4. What is your understanding of the "trust bank" metaphor? Does it make sense to you? Why or why not?

5. Have you ever experienced a relationship where the other person emptied the trust bank of your relationship? What happened and was the trust account restored in any way?

Conclusion

Unwrapping Your Gift and
Numbers 6:24–26

To love another person is to see the face of God.[1]
—*Les Misérables*, the Musical

THIS ENTIRE BOOK HAS BEEN BASED on the premise that language is a gift, given to us from God as part of being made in his image. Learning how to use that gift involves a journey filled with ups and downs. I have encouraged you to use the lens of communication theory combined with the lens of Scripture to "see" the gift more clearly to help you navigate your journey. In the first chapter of this book, I argued how humans have been created with the gift of language. This gift, rife with barriers and challenges, is not a mistake. Communication scholars have studied, examined, dissected, and explored this gift for centuries to better understand it. As I have studied the gift over the years, my own faith journey has allowed me to see that Scripture is filled with valuable tools and insights on how to navigate language and communication. This book is an attempt to put some of those insights in writing to share with you. I wish I could write that I have mastered the gift of language and communication and that my life is an example of perfect communication. Far from it. My life is filled with flaws and challenges like everybody else. Just ask my family and friends. They will gladly share with you the areas of my life that need work. What I have shared in this book are a few of the tools I have learned along the way to avoid mismanaging my gift of language and communication as best I can.

This book has provided you with several common topic areas studied in interpersonal communication. Each topic was unwrapped through the lens of a communication theory and combined with the lens of a biblical reference to show God's plan for how to use your gift. My prayer is that by having read this book, you now have more resources to draw upon when you unwrap your gift. It will take some time and work and honest effort on your part to undo some old negative communication habits that may be weighing you down. I am praying that this book gives you some hope by showing you that there are ways to undo bad habits and form new habits that can honor God.

My heart always feels heavy whenever I hear of a relationship being damaged or terminated because of communication problems. I know the pain that comes from this hurt based on the personal experience of my own failures. God made us to be relational beings. He gave us our gift of language and communication so we could have relationships. So, when relationships struggle because of problems with the gift, I struggle to see how that is God's plan. But I have argued in this book that the biggest barrier to improving our language skills tends to be our pride.

It can be hard sometimes to take responsibility for the mismanagement of your gift. The key to keep in mind is that the challenge is often just a lack of knowledge and appropriate tools. The problem is not necessarily a character flaw that you cannot address. Your communication tools were taught to you. That means you can un-teach bad habits or poor tools you have developed, and work to replace them with new, better tools of communication.

I have tried with each chapter to provide some tools you can use to improve the use of your gift. These tools will only work if you are willing to admit you have some areas in your life that need some work. That is not easy. I know this from personal experience. My pride has caused plenty of relationship problems in my life. My prayer for you is that you can open your heart to the tools in this book along with praying for God's wisdom and help so you can improve how you use your gift. Every tool provided in this book works best when both parties in a relationship are committed to practicing a particular principle or idea together. Some of the communication skills in this book can work from a one-sided perspective, but there is a point when one person can no longer carry the load. Therefore, it is my hope and prayer that you will share this book with someone you believe would benefit from working together with you on applying and practicing some of the skills in this book.

One of my favorite books is Victor Hugo's *Les Misérables*. Set during the French Revolution, this story of love, relationships, forgiveness, and reconciliation is matched by little else I have ever read outside of the Bible. When the book was turned into a Broadway musical and a movie, those productions quickly became my favorites in those genres as well. The story explored the life of a man, Jean Valjean, who was unfairly imprisoned for 19 years of hard labor for stealing a loaf of bread. While on parole, Valjean again stole from a Bishop of the church, who forgave him, but admonished him to turn his life around. Valjean made good with his life, eventually caring for a young woman, Fantine, who worked in one of his factories. Upon her death, Fantine begged Valjean to take care of her daughter, Cosette. He agreed and spent the rest of his life caring for Cosette. In the stage and film versions of the book, upon his death, Jean Valjean is led into paradise by the spirit of Fantine and the Bishop who forgave him. Together they all sing the epilogue of the story which includes the message, "To love another person is to see the face of God."[2]

I find the theology in these lyrics to be profound. As people of faith, seeking and knowing God drives us to learn about him. In Chapter 8, I explored the topic of listening and made the argument that since God is love and God listens, then listening is loving. When we listen to someone and do so in a way that honors God, then we can love that person, even if that person is unlovable. When we love others, God is pleased. Thus, as Valjean, Fantine, and the Bishop sang, when we love another person using our language and communication skills, we are able to see the face of God.

As you finish this book, my prayer for you is that you have clearer lenses now to look through as you unwrap your gift while you are on your journey. As you navigate your journey, I hope these new lenses will allow you to see the face of God in your daily communication.

• A Blessing to be Poured Out Upon You and • Your Gift of Communication

"The Lord bless you and keep you;
the Lord make his face shine on you and be gracious to you;
the Lord turn his face toward you and give you peace."
(Numbers 6:24-26)

Notes

Introduction

[1] Stephen R. Covey, *The 7 Habits of Highly Effective People* (New York: Simon & Schuster, 1989), 137.

[2] Quentin J. Schultze, *Communicating with Grace and Virtue: Learning to Listen, Speak, Text, and Interact as a Christian* (Grand Rapids, MI: Baker, 2020), 22.

[3] Ibid., 22 (italics mine).

[4] Brian H. Sptizberg and William R. Cupach, *The Dark Side of Interpersonal Communication* (Hillsdale, NJ: Lawrence Erlbaum, 1994), 25–50.

[5] Tim Muehlhoff and Todd Lewis, *Authentic Communication: Christian Speech Engaging Culture* (Downers Grove, IL: InterVarsity, 2010), 38.

Chapter 1

[1] Truth Devour, *Wantin* (Publiscious Book Publishing, 2013), 198.

[2] James Strong, *Strong's Exhaustive Concordance* (Nashville, TN: Crusade Bible), 52 (Hebrew and Chaldee Dictionary).

[3] Gregory Radick, *The Simian Tongue: The Long Debate About Animal Language* (Chicago: University of Chicago Press, 2007), 8.

[4] Thom Scott-Phillips, *Speaking Our Minds: Why Human Communication is Different, and How Language Evolved to Make it Special* (New York: Palgrave Macmillan, 2015), 154.

[5] Charles Darwin, *On the Origin of Species* (London: John Murray, 1859).

[6] Max Müller, "Lectures on Mr. Darwin's Philosophy of Language," May 1873, *Frazer's Magazine*, 7–8, 147–233.

[7] Ibid., 183.

[8] Luella Agger Kellogg and Winthrop Niles Kellogg, *The Ape and the Child: A Comparative Study of the Environmental Influence Upon Early Behavior* (New York: Hafner Publishing Co., 1933), 385.

[9] Stephen R. Anderson, *Doctor Dolittle's Delusion: Animals and the Uniqueness of Human Language* (New Haven, CT: Yale University Press, 2006); Richard Lynch Garner, *The Speech of Monkeys* (London: William Heinemann, 1892); Gregory Radick, *The Simian Tongue: The Long Debate About Animal Language* (Chicago: University of Chicago Press, 2007).

[10] Joseph Berger, "Chasing a Name Lost to Time," *The New York Times*, July 2,

2011, https://archive.nytimes.com/cityroom.blogs.nytimes.com/2011/07/02/chasing-a-name-lost-to-time-2/.

[11] Herbert S. Terrace, Laura-Ann Petitto, Richard Sanders, and Thomas G. Bever, "Can an Ape Create a Sentence?" *Science* 206, no. 4421 (November 23, 1979): 891–902.

[12] Herbert S. Terrace, *Why Chimpanzees Can't Learn Language and Only Humans Can* (New York: Columbia University Press, 2019).

[13] Scott-Phillips, *Speaking Our Minds*, 80.

[14] W. Tecumseh Fitch, *The Evolution of Language* (Cambridge: Cambridge University Press, 2010), 140.

[15] James R. Hurford, *Origins of Grammar: Language in the Light of Evolution* (Oxford: Oxford University Press, 2011), 260.

[16] Scott-Phillips, *Speaking Our Minds*, 4.

[17] Steven Green and Peter Marler, "The Analysis of Animal Communication," in *Handbook of Behavioral Neurobiology*, eds. Peter Marler and J. G. Vandenbergh (New York: Plenum, 1979), 73–158.

[18] Scott-Phillips, *Speaking Our Minds*, 6.

[19] Fred C. Dyer, "The Biology of the Dance Language, *Annual Review of Entomology* 47 (January 2002): 917–949.

[20] Scott-Phillips, *Speaking Our Minds*, 25.

[21] Susan Langer, "Language and Thought," in *Language Awareness: Readings for College Writers*, 10th edition, eds. Paul Eschholz and Alfred Rosa (Boston: Bedford/St. Martins, 2009), 77.

[22] Ibid., 77–78.

[23] Ibid., 78–79.

[24] Virginia Clark, Paul Eschholz, and Alfred Rosa, *Language: Readings in Language and Culture* (New York: St. Martins, 1998), 75

[25] Ibid., 76.

[26] Ibid., 77.

[27] Ibid.

[28] Scott-Phillips, *Speaking Our Minds*, 11.

[29] Phillip Lieberman, "The Evolution of Human Speech," *Current Anthropology* 48 (2007): 39–66.

[30] Mary Duenwald, "The Biology of Baby-Talk: Why Scientists go gaga over infants goos-goos," *Discover* 25 (December 2003), https://www.discovermagazine.com/magazine/2003/december.

[31] Why Study Communication? Pathways to your Future. National Communication Association. https://www.natcom.org/academic-professional-resources/why-study-communication

[32] 1 John 1:9, King James Version.

Chapter 2

[1] Virginia Satir, *The New Peoplemaking* (University of California: Science and Behavior Books, 1988), 1.

[2] Thomas Hobbes, *Leviathan* (New York: Penguin Classics, 2017), 100.

[3] I have designed these elements as my own interpretation of the communication process based on research from the following sources and area of application: Ronald

Adler, Lawrence Rosenfeld, and Russell Proctor II, *Interplay: The Process of Interpersonal Communication*, 13th edition (New York: Oxford, 2014), 10 (Transactional nature of communication); Johnnye Akin, Alvin Goldberg, Gail Myers, and Joseph Stewart, eds., "A Transactional Model of Communication," *Language Behavior* 41 (1970): 43–61 (Transactional nature of communication); Dean C. Barnlund, "A Transactional Model of Communication," in *Foundation of Communication Theory*, Kenneth K. and C. David Mortensen, eds. (New York: Harper Row, 1970), 83–102 (Transactional nature of communication); Ross Buck and C. Arthur Vanlear, "Verbal and Nonverbal Communication: Distinguishing Symbolic, Spontaneous, and Pseudo-Spontaneous Nonverbal Behavior," *Journal of Communication* 52 (2002): 522–542 (Unintentional behavior), (Transactional nature of communication); Gwen A. Hullman, "Communicative Adaptability Scale: Evaluating Its Use as an 'Other Report' Measure," *Communication Reports* 20 (2007): 51–74 (Adaptability of communication); Brian H. Spitzberg, "An Examination of Trait Measures of Interpersonal Competence," *Communication Reports* 4 (1991): 22–29 (Situational nature of communication); Paul Watzlawick, Janet Beavin Baveles, and Don D. Jackson, *Pragmatics of Human Communication: A Study of Interactional Patterns, Pathologies, and Paradoxes* (New York: Norton, 1967) (Relational dimension of communication).

[4] John Stewart, ed. *Bridges Not Walls: A Book About Interpersonal Communication* (New York: McGraw Hill, 2009), 20.

[5] Ibid., 17.

[6] Proverbs 6:16–19: "There are six things the Lord hates, seven that are detestable to him: haughty eyes, a lying tongue, hands that shed innocent blood, a heart that devises wicked schemes, feet that are quick to rush into evil, a false witness who pours out lies and a person who stirs up conflict in the community."

Chapter 3

[1] Emily K. Asencio, "Self-Esteem, Reflected Appraisals, and Self-Views: Examining Criminal and Work Identities, *Social Psychology Quarterly* 76, no. 4 (2013): 291–313.

[2] Ronald Adler, Lawrence Rosenfeld, and Russell Proctor II, *Interplay: The Process of Interpersonal Communication*, 13th edition (New York: Oxford, 2014), 90.

[3] E. P. Lemay and K. L. Dudley, "Implication of Reflected Appraisals on Interpersonal Insecurity for Suspicion and Power. *Personality and Social Psychology Bulletin* 35 (2009): 1672–1686.

[4] Harry M. Wallace and Dianne M. Tice, "Reflected Appraisal through a 21st-Century Looking Glass," in *Handbook of Self and Identity* 2nd edition, eds. Mark R. Leary and June Price Tangney (New York: Guilford, 2012), 124–140.

[5] "haimorrheo"—"To flow blood," in James Strong, *Strong's Exhaustive Concordance* (Nashville, TN: Crusade Bible), 8.

[6] Elizabeth W. Goldstein, *Impurity and Gender in the Hebrew Bible* (New York: Lexington Books, 2015), 31–45.

[7] Jacob Milgrom, "Leviticus 1–16: A New Translation with Introduction and Commentary," in *The Anchor Bible 3* (New York: Doubleday, 1991), 124.

Chapter 4

[1] Joel Porte, ed., *Emerson in his Journals* (Cambridge, MA: Harvard University Press, 1982), 514.

[2] Leon Festinger, *A Theory of Cognitive Dissonance* (Stanford, CA: Stanford University Press, 1957), 2.

[3] Em Griffin, *A First Look at Communication Theory*, 7th edition (Boston: McGraw-Hill, 2008), 205.

[4] Ibid.

[5] Festinger, *A Theory of Cognitive Dissonance*, 84–97.

[6] Andreas Kappes, Ann H. Harvey, Terry Lohrenz, P Read Montague, and Tali Sharot, "Confirmation Bias in the Utilization of Others' Opinion Strength," *Nature Neuroscience* 23 (2020): 130–137.

[7] Adam Clarke, *Adam Clarke's Commentary on the Bible* (Grand Rapids, MI: Baker, 1967), 872.

[8] See Matthew 12:36.

Chapter 5

[1] Mamutty Chola, *Pearls of Wisdom* (Mumbai, India, BecomeShakespeare.com 2019), 280.

[2] Colleen Hoover, *Maybe Someday* Book 1 (New York: Atria, 2014), 308.

[3] Steven L. Gordon, "Social Structural Effects on Emotion," in Theodore D. Kemper, ed., *Agenda in the Sociology of Emotion* (Albany, NY: State University of New York, 1990), 145–179.

[4] While I did not ask him that question, I did leave the retreat that night and went home early.

[5] Daniel Goleman, *Emotional Intelligence: Why it Can Matter More Than IQ* (New York: Bantam, 1995), 115.

[6] Exodus 32:22.

[7] Matthew 3:16–17.

[8] Matthew 27:46, 26:39, and Luke 11:46.

[9] Matthew 16:23, 21:12–13.

[10] Matthew 26:38, Mark 14:34, and John 11:35.

[11] Matthew 26:40.

[12] Matthew 28:63.

[13] Matthew 26:42.

[14] Matthew 23:13–29, Mark 1:25, 8:32, and Luke 9:55.

[15] Mark 3:5.

[16] Mark 9:19.

[17] Mark 10:14.

[18] Mark 8:12, John 11:33.

[19] Luke 7:13, John 8:11, and John 11:38.

[20] Luke 22:44.

[21] Psalm 25:6, 27:7, 18:50, 37:26, 57:1, 59:10, 85:7, 89:1, 101:1, 103:8, 136:1–26.

[22] Psalm 26:3, 31:21, 36:7, 68:3, 89:33, 92:2.

[23] Psalm 7:6, 7:11, 30:5, 78:31, 80:4, 85:5, and 106:40.

[24] Psalm 18:35.
[25] Psalm 36.
[26] Psalm 149:4.
[27] Psalm 145:8.
[28] Psalm 4:1.
[29] Psalm 13:2, 18:4, 116:3.
[30] Psalm 16:9, 71:14, 78:7, 147:11.
[31] Psalm 16:11.
[32] Psalm 22:1.
[33] Psalm 23:4, 55:5, 72:5, 118:6, 147:11.
[34] Psalm 37:8.
[35] Psalm 38.
[36] Psalm 42.
[37] Psalm 44:6, 56:4.
[38] Psalm 69:19, 119:6, 119:78.
[39] Psalm 88:9.
[40] Psalm 112:1, 119:35.
[41] Psalm 118:5,120:1.
[42] Psalm 127:5, 146:5.
[43] Ronald Adler, Lawrence Rosenfeld, and Russell Proctor II, *Interplay: The Process of Interpersonal Communication*, 13th edition (New York: Oxford, 2014), 159.
[44] A. Ellis and D. Ellis, "Rational Emotive Behavior Therapy," in Gary R. VandenBos, Edward B. Meidenbauer, and Julia Frank-Mcneil, eds., *Psychotherapy Theories and Techniques: A Reader* (Washington, DC: American Psychological Association, 2014), 289.

Chapter 6

[1] Ezra Pound, *ABC of Reading* (New York: New Direction Books, 2010), 34.
[2] Ronald Adler, Lawrence Rosenfeld, and Russell Proctor II, *Interplay: The Process of Interpersonal Communication*, 13th edition (New York: Oxford, 2014), 144.
[3] Meaning "would there be any extra credit questions on the test?" or "Do you have any *lagniappe* for my potatoes?" meaning "gravy."
[4] Ronald Adler, et al., *Interplay*, 144.
[5] Deborah Tannen, *You Just Don't Understand: Women and Men in Conversation* (New York: Ballantine, 1990), 74.
[6] Ibid., 24.
[7] Cultural linguist Walter Ong refers to this type of language use as "Agonisms." Walter J. Ong, *Fighting for Life: Contest, Sexuality, and Consciousness* (Ithaca, NY: Cornell, 1981), in Deborah Tannen, *You Just Don't Understand: Women and Men in Conversation* (New York: Ballantine, 1990), 150.
[8] Tannen, *You Just Don't Understand*, 25.
[9] The word "tongue" in Greek means "language" and "one that is acquired" (learned). James Strong, *Strong's Exhaustive Concordance* (Nashville, TN: Crusade Bible), 20.

Chapter 7

[1] Sylvia Plath, *The Bell Jar* (New York: Faber and Faber, 1978), 153.

[2] Donald Miller, *A Million Miles in a Thousand Years: What I learned While Editing My Life* (Nashville, TN: Thomas Nelson, 2009), 61.

[3] He always notified the Registrar's Office of what he was doing, and they would encourage the student to wait and see how the second- or third-class sessions went.

[4] Judee K. Burgoon, "A Communication Model of Personal Space Violations: Explication and an Initial Test," *Human Communication Research* 4 (1978): 129–142.

[5] Richard West and Lynn Turner, *Introducing Communication Theory: Analysis and Application*, 5th edition (New York: McGraw Hill Education, 2014), 126.

[6] Fred E. Jandt, *An Introduction to Intercultural Communication: Identities in a Global Community* (Thousand Oaks, CA: Sage, 2021), 113.

[7] West and Turner, *Introducing Communication Theory*, 134–135.

[8] Mark 2:13–17, King James Version.

[9] Luke 19:1–10, King James Version. Jesus associated with tax collectors who were agents of the Roman Empire, who typically demanded a higher amount than the law required and pocketed the difference.

[10] Mark 1:16–20, King James Version.

[11] Luke 7:1–10, John 11:1–44, King James Version.

[12] Matthew 12:1–8, King James Version.

[13] Adam Clarke, *Adam Clarke's Commentary on the Bible* (Grand Rapids, MI: Baker, 1967), 936.

Chapter 8

[1] There is a great deal of disagreement over which Greek philosopher said this quote, different publications have attributed it to Diogenes, Zeno, Epictetus, and Socrates. For the purposes of this book I will cite: Michael Hammond, *Parenting Difficult Children: Strategies for Parents of Preschoolers to Preteens* (New York: Rowen and Littlefield, 2014), 80.

[2] Ronald Adler, Lawrence Rosenfeld, and Russell Proctor II, *Interplay: The Process of Interpersonal Communication*, 13th edition (New York: Oxford, 2014), 211.

[3] Ibid., 224.

[4] Stephen R. Covey, *The 7 Habits of Highly Effective People* (New York: Simon & Schuster, 1989), 251.

[5] Quentin J. Schultze and Diane M. Badzinski, *An Essential Guide to Interpersonal Communication: Building Great Relationships with Faith, Skill, and Virtue in the Age of Social Media* (Grand Rapids, MI: Baker, 2015), 15.

Chapter 9

[1] Samuel White III, *Hope for Your Soul: Words of Encouragement* (Bloomington, IN: WestBow Press, 2018), 95.

[2] Richard West and Lynn Turner, *Introducing Communication Theory: Analysis and Application* 5th Edition (New York: McGraw Hill Education, 2014), 164–178.

[3] Henry Cloud and John Townson, *Boundaries: When to Say Yes, When to Say No,*

To Take Control of Your Life (Grand Rapids, MI: Zondervan Publishing House, 1992), 27–48.

⁴ Matthew 25:31–46.

Chapter 10

¹ Haim G. Ginott, *Teacher and Child: A Book for Parents and Teachers* (New York: Avon Books, 1972), 66.

² Kevin R. Betts and Verlin B. Hinsz, "Group Marginalization: Extending Research on Interpersonal Rejection to Small Groups," *Personality & Social Psychology Review* 17 (2013): 355–370.

³ René M. Daily, "Testing Components of Confirmation: How Acceptance and Challenge from Mothers, Fathers, and Siblings are Related to Adolescent Self-Concept," *Communication Monographs* 77 (2010): 592–617.

⁴ Ephesians 4:29, King James Version.

⁵ John 15:12.

⁶ Chapter 12 will explore the claim that God made us to be conflictual beings.

⁷ Proverbs 6:16–17, King James Version.

⁸ John Gottman, "Why Marriages Fail" in Kathleen M. Galvin and Pamela J. Cooper, eds., *Making Connections: Readings in Relational Communication* (Los Angeles, CA: Roxbury, 2003), 258–266.

⁹ 2 Corinthians 5:17.

Chapter 11

¹ Fredrick Backman, *Beartown: A Novel* (New York: Washington Square Press, 2018), 273.

² Thich Nhat Hanh, *Anger: Wisdom for Cooling the Flames* (New York: Riverhead Books, 2002), 55.

³ See Chapter 10 in this book.

⁴ See Chapter 2 in this book.

⁵ See Chapter 10 in this book.

⁶ John Gottman, *Why Marriages Succeed or Fail and How You Can Make Yours Last* (New York: Simon & Schuster, 1994), 258–266.

⁷ See Chapter 12 in this book for a more in-depth explanation of the harm in name-calling.

⁸ See Chapter 10 for detailed explanation of confirming versus disconfirming language choice.

⁹ Ronald Adler, Lawrence Rosenfeld, and Russell Proctor II, *Interplay: The Process of Interpersonal Communication*, 13ᵗʰ edition (New York: Oxford, 2014), 383.

¹⁰ Mutually agreed upon "time-outs" are different if both parties have agreed to walk away and have a cooling down period. But both parties must agree.

Chapter 12

¹ Katharine Graham, *Personal History* (New York: Alfred A. Knopf, 1997), 532.

[2] Steve Chalke, *Change Agents: 25 Hard-Learned Lessons in the Art of Getting Things Done* (Grand Rapids, MI: Zondervan, 2007), 23.

[3] Frank L. Gardner and Zella E. Moore, "Understanding Clinical Anger and Violence: The Anger Avoidance Model," *Behavior Modification* 32 (2008): 897–912.

[4] Ibid., 903. See also Charles Carver and Eddie Harmon-Jones, "Anger is an Approach-Related Affect: Evidence and Implications," *Psychological Bulletin* 135 (2009): 183–204; Jennifer S. Lerner and Dacher Keltner, "Fear, Anger, and Risk," *Journal of Personality and Social Psychology* 81 (2001): 146–159; Thomas Scheff, "Toward Defining Basic Emotions," *Qualitative Inquiry* 21 (2015): 111–121; Janne Van Doorn, Marcel Zeelenberg, and Seger M. Breugelman, "Anger and Prosocial Behavior," *Emotion Review* 6 (2014): 261–268.

[5] For examples see Exodus 32:22, Deuteronomy 1:37, Psalm 7:11, or Isaiah 5:25 King James Version.

[6] See Matthew 21:12–17 or Mark 3:5.

[7] Or any other vile name I could call him (you fill in the blank with any name you call someone).

[8] Jean-Philippe Laurenceau, Lisa Feldman Barrett, and Michael J. Rovine, "The Interpersonal Process Model of Intimacy in Marriage: A Daily-Diary and Multilevel Modeling Approach," *Journal of Family Psychology* 19 (2005): 314–323; E. M. Waring, "Facilitating Marital Intimacy through Self-Disclosure," *American Journal of Family Therapy* 9 (1981): 33–42.

[9] Stephen R. Covey, *The 7 Habits of Highly Effective People* (New York: Simon & Schuster, 1989), 188–190.

Conclusion

[1] Herbert Kretzmer, "Finale," recorded and mixed at CTS Studios, Wembly, England on *Les Miserables: The Musical Sensation*, CD.

[2] Ibid.

Scripture Index

Subject Index

www.ingramcontent.com/pod-product-compliance
Lightning Source LLC
Chambersburg PA
CBHW032054040426
42335CB00037B/712